# Work: Inspiration and Transformation

GW00760138

## About the Author

Andrée Harpur, a Masters graduate from UCD, has been involved in the area of Career Guidance for the past fifteen years. In her private practice, based in Dublin, she deals with people of all ages, from school and college students to adults who wish to examine and re-assess their careers. She also works in a consultancy capacity for various financial institutions and government bodies. She has contributed to *The Irish Times* and has taken part in discussions on work and careers on both radio and television in Ireland.

# Work: Inspiration and Transformation

Andrée Harpur

BLACKHALL
*Publishing*

This book was typeset by
Gough Typesetting Services for
BLACKHALL PUBLISHING
26 Eustace Street
Dublin 2
Ireland
e-mail: blackhall@tinet.ie

ISBN: 1 901657 22 1

A catalogue record for this book is available
from the British Library.

Printed in Ireland
by Betaprint.

*Dedication*

To Des, Joshua, Matthew, Vicky and Joanne

# Acknowledgements

❖ To my family for their constant encouragement.

❖ To Anne Harpur who helped me believe in myself when my spirit flagged.

❖ To Tony Mason, my publisher, whose clear-sighted vision and in-depth knowledge of this area made sure that this book actually happened.

❖ To Jane Harrison for her infinite patience and skill in putting this text together.

❖ To Nuella Murnaghan for her creative input.

❖ To Louise Neiland, artist, for a wonderful logo.

❖ To Áine Keenan for her wonderfully inspiring thoughts. She has greatly influenced this book.

# Contents

# Foreword

A consequence of professional counselling psychology courses in the UK and Ireland, and in the broader field of counselling and psychotherapy, has been the status accorded to career counselling. It is very much perceived as a peripheral activity, heavily laden with information seeking and receiving, and involving simple matching of person to job. This perception is also unfortunately the popular fiction with representative organisations such as the Irish Association for Counselling and Therapy. The counter trend is the burgeoning field of occupational and organisational psychology as evidenced in the increasing number of psychologists who are members of the Division of Occupational Psychology in the British Psychological Society. Career counselling bridges both camps.

Another phenomenon of the field is how poorly the adult population, particularly those active in the workplace or who have the potential to be so, is provided with career counselling facilities both of a public and private nature. When we consider that workplace activity takes up at least half of one's waking hours and that the active adult population is on average twice as large as the school and college-going segment, the lack of provision of career counselling services is all the more frightening. Part of the reason for this lack is that the benefits of career counselling have not been elaborated clearly enough; neither is there any general insight into what actually happens during career counselling and there are few records of what outcomes have occurred, particularly over time.

Andrée Harpur's book is a remarkable contribution to dispensing the clouds around the process, outcomes and benefits of career counselling. It is as sensitively written as Andrée's clients were sensitively counselled by her. The case studies presented throughout the book highlight how many facets of decision-making and career behaviour are psychological events. They show how intricately our self-image, personal values and practical family considerations and expectations are intertwined; how the workplace culture, values, expectations and behaviour present major challenges to the latter set of factors; how bewildering these challenges become for adults; how personal dreams, ideals, hopes and aspirations become buried but can be successfully resurrected.

One of the leading theorists in the field of counselling psychology over the past 30 years, John Krumboltz, has stated: "Career counselling is the most complex type of counselling because the counsellor must possess all the skills of other counsellors, and in addition, know employment trends, methods of preparation for various work roles, career assessment techniques and methods for changing work-related behaviour, emotions and cognitives." Andrée and her clients have given their experiences to us, illustrating exactly what Krumboltz means.

This book will be of tremendous value to adults experiencing self-doubt in relation to the workplace, giving them the courage to make the first step to benefit from career counselling.

John McCarthy
Director
National Centre for Guidance in Education
Dublin, August 1998

# Introduction

The main object of this book is to dispel a number of myths that are currently circulating about careers. The first message that most of us receive is that if we work very hard and put all our effort into seeking the perfect job or the perfect career, that on attaining this we will be perfectly happy. It is important for all of us to find a job which fulfils us and in which we can use our natural talents. It is also of vital importance to us that our basic needs are met and that we can live comfortably on the salary we earn.

However, in my years of practice, I have frequently come across people who have reached the top of the ladder and even though their material needs are met they are still asking some deep and searching questions. There still exist some other deeper needs which are not met. One man explained to me that he had put 20 years of his life into climbing up each rung of the corporate ladder and when he reached the top he realised that his journey was not complete – but he didn't have any more rungs to climb. There was obviously a different direction in which this man needed to travel.

The second message that we are given is that everybody else seems to have the answer, everybody else seems to know a secret technique to which we are not privy. We feel that, because we are not successful in our career, it is simply because we haven't found the method, we haven't learned the technique. However, in this book, it will become clear that there is no fixed method, there is no stated technique. We will see that we cannot borrow somebody else's path and follow it. The only valid path for us is our own.

We shall hear about many people who have faced different challenges in their careers. These challenges have caused many problems and have made these individuals very isolated and alone. We shall find that each of these people felt that there were no rules that they could follow, no procedures to which they could refer. However, when they paused and stepped back from the situation, they realised that there were many more things on which they could rely, but which they have never recognised before. They realised that they had deep and innate talents which could enrich their present experience and could also contribute hugely to their work situation. Bit-by-bit, they realised that their work had meaning and that their own personal gifts and talents could be used in the workplace. They found out that these natural gifts could not only be used, but were very valuable.

In many cases, these people had to go beyond the obvious and ask deeper questions (such as "Who am I?" and "Why am I here?"). These questions, from the outset, seem to be very small and very simple, but they embark us on a fairly lengthy process of self-discovery. We learn that the process is on-going and progresses day-by-day. However, once we become in touch with our own natural talents and gifts, we never forget them and look for opportunities every day in which to use them. We begin to appreciate ourselves just as we are and to know that this identity is valuable.

You will notice that this book is not based on scientific, empirical evidence, nor does it draw on results of scientific or psychological studies. The information is gained purely from my own personal experience from many years as a careers consultant. The case studies that are included are the stories of actual clients I have advised over the years – though, obviously, their identities have been changed to maintain confidentiality.

I do hope, however, that their experiences in the workplace will be useful to you, the reader. Even though you may not have encountered exactly the same situations, perhaps you will be inspired by the courage and the tenacity of the people in this book.

I have also found it necessary to include some cases which have not seemingly worked, in which people have not, for various reasons, continued the process. I do not consider this in any way to have been a failure, it can be just as profitable for us to learn what we are not willing to do as it is to learn what we are willing to do. I also included these cases to show you that this is based on real life and that life is not always predictable. The outcome of many of my cases I cannot predict and I always realise that the outcome is never solely within my power. I try to provide my clients with a safe and relatively structured space in which they can step back from their work situation and ask pertinent questions. The psychometric tests that I use can provide an objective and valuable springboard from which to commence this investigation. However, the knowledge gained from the subsequent deeper questions we ask is based solely upon the client's perception of him or herself and the position that they see themselves occupying in the world.

In this way, in this book, we do not view work as being separated from the person's life, nor do we see life as being separated from the workplace. We also view the individual as being an integral part of society and that any contribution that this individual makes is ultimately meaningful and contributes a great deal to both the workplace and the community at large.

In describing each of these cases, I make no attempt to suggest that there is a specific method or a specific technique to be used in any situation. The main point of this book is to show how each individual reacted in a way that reflects their own personality, gifts and talents. The method adopted by each of these people, may not necessarily be valid for another person. What this book does hope to reflect is the integrity of each of these people and the hope that this very integrity may be inspirational to others.

This book is not written to produce any guidelines, it is written more to inspire us to have the courage to rely upon ourselves and to know that the knowledge we have to contribute to the world is valid and can be trusted. I hope to identify some of the most fearful questions in order to render them less frightening and to introduce the reader to people who have tried to answer these questions in their own lives. More importantly, this book aims to reassure you that if you are thinking of embarking on this search and asking these questions, you are not alone. A great many people have trodden this path before you.

This process is not about solving your life problems or about finding the one job which will mean you will be happy for as long as you live. It is about discovering that we already have the answers to the questions we ask. We do not need to depend on others and we can always have control over our work, even when it seems that we do not. This process is simply about waking up to the fact that we already have all of the skills that we need. All we need is a little help with our confidence to be able to use them.

Once people get a taste of this confidence and actually see it in action in their own workplace, they are ready to go it alone. Awakening to our true potential is not a long process, but developing it and integrating it in a harmonious way into the rest of our lives is the work of a lifetime. All of the questions need not be answered in one day.

# ONE

# The First Session: "What am I doing Here?"

It is often said that the most difficult part of the journey is the first step. This is certainly true in the area of careers consultancy. Most sessions begin with a client asking the question, "What am I doing here, I haven't really a clue?" They explain to me that when they first rang, they were full of enthusiasm but that now the time for the appointment has come, they were about to ring me and cancel. However, something made them go through with the process. Even then, they are full of fear and self-doubt.

The vast majority of us find the process of assessment very daunting. It brings us back to our school days when we could fail tests and usually get into a lot of trouble. We also have a fear that it is something to do with being judged "good enough" or "not good enough". Some of my clients hesitate when I tell them of the process. They are not quite sure whether they want to do that to themselves, especially when it is voluntary and in their spare time!

Most clients are afraid to do the interest inventory in case they find out that they are interested in nothing. I have never found this. Everybody is interested in something, and usually clients are interested in many areas at the one time. They are also afraid to do aptitude tests in case they find out that they have no intelligence. However, I assure them from the outset that it is absolutely impossible not to be "intelligent". It is simply a question of finding out with which intelligence we are most comfortable. But perhaps it is the area of the personality profile which makes most of them hesitate. It is precisely because they are not acquainted with the process that we are afraid of it. Some people say to me, "I don't know, God knows what problems this will uncover!" It is important to know that the process is not about uncovering "problems" but about identifying "preferred ways of behaving".

When we can identify the personality characteristics that we most enjoy using in the workplace, we can then begin to draw a picture of the work atmosphere in which we are most comfortable. Generally, people find the whole area of self-knowledge fascinating and when clients have finished the profile, it is generally the case that they found it fun and informative.

Another great fear that most clients have is the difficulty in defining where to begin their questioning. They find it difficult to actually explain what brought them to this process. I have found that most careers research starts with a niggling feeling that all is not as well as it could be. It is an empty feeling that is hard to define and even harder to justify. When we are asked exactly what we want, we reply in terms of, "I just feel that I could be *living* my life more." Because we find it hard to clarify what we want, we also find it hard to know what to do about it.

The question of career exploration is made even more difficult by the fact that a change of job can very often signal a whole change in lifestyle. It does not only affect us, it also affects those close to us – some of whom may depend totally on that cheque we bring in each month.

When we get over the fear, we then face the guilt – if we have jobs, aren't we lucky? Why are we still looking? It is hard to tell ourselves that we have a right to be happy and that we can do work that we love and even get paid for it!

The next step we face is confusion. Where do I start? Do I even know what I am looking for? In this area, there are tools to help us in the form of interest inventories and personality questionnaires. The former helps us to identify the general career which may motivate us and the latter identifies the general personality characteristics we are comfortable using in the workplace and those we would rather not use. These questionnaires are not definitive but they can and do act as a solid, structured basis for further questioning.

The objective of this book is to demonstrate that such a search can be carried out successfully, despite all the possible impediments. All of these questions need not be answered in one day. Why are we rushing? We have a lifetime to answer these questions. We are involved in a process which unfolds step-by-step.

This process involves us asking the question, "Why am I doing the job that I am now doing?" We choose the work we do for a large variety of reasons. Most reasons were, at the time, perfectly valid. We may have felt that we had no choice but to work. Any job would do, as one job is as good as another. We may have been conscious of the amount of money we earn and felt that we needed to earn a large amount to make ourselves feel important in our own lives and in the lives of others. To increase our need for self-esteem, we may have chosen a position with power and status. In this way, we felt that we would ensure that people would have a positive impression of us and in so doing, we felt good about ourselves. Our job conferred on us the external image we felt we needed to feel safe in the world. We were prepared to work and to do whatever it took because, for the moment, all of our needs were met.

For a while, satisfying these external needs was sufficient. However, after some time, we may have begun to wonder whether fulfilling the needs of others actually means that we are fulfilling our own needs. While we were impressing others, were we actually boring ourselves? Were we spending too much time doing things that we felt we should do, while our real selves were yearning for a different expression? We may have begun to experience an itch – gentle but persistent. It only surfaced now and again but asked disturbing little questions, "Is this all I am ever going to do?" or "Am I really happy doing this?" We mainly ignored this little voice because it was not logical and severely disturbed the security we had so painstakingly built up.

But for some of us, this situation became so intolerable that we had to look at these questions more closely. We may have realised that we felt that we had no control in relation to our work. We saw that we had no clear notion as to why we were doing the job we were doing in the first place and had no idea what we wanted to achieve while doing it.

We chose our job with little regard to the intelligence with which we were most comfortable. We had little idea what motivated us, so we looked to the workplace to provide us with that motivation. We had also taken little account of our personal characteristics. We assessed what type of person the job required us to be and then tried to squeeze ourselves into that mould. We had basically put the cart before the horse. We had taken all the requirements of the workplace and interpreted them as our requirements. We had never, in the first place, assessed ourselves to find out what our requirements were on a deeper level.

Yet, even though we were well aware that something serious was amiss, we may have tried to rationalise the fact that we did not need to change. "I am actually very comfortable the way I am." "My job is really not that bad." "I am lucky, there are so many so worse off than I am." These arguments worked for a while and then the small voice came back. We told ourselves that it was stupid to be in our thirties and still not to know what we were doing. If the perfect job came along, we may not even recognise it. We may have told ourselves that this "career exploration thing" only works for kids in school. Not for adults. Then we meet with the 70 year old who is still living a full and challenging life and we think, maybe the right time is now! We may not have known what we wanted, but we had a clear idea of what we did not want.

But the prospect of change is, for the majority of us, an absolutely terrifying one. We think, "What if I change and end up far worse than I am now with no prospect of a job at all?"

I explain to my clients that coming to a careers consultation is working in the realm of ideas. I explain to them that it is as if they were given a gold credit card with an unlimited budget and then they were asked to go into a very expensive shop. They had the complete freedom to try on anything they wanted in that shop and to examine how each outfit looked on themselves. However, they were under absolutely no obligation to buy. They could take as long as they wanted to look, to decide and to gather more knowledge but they did not have to take that decision to buy. This is very similar to the careers consultation. It is a safe space in which we can look at many different ideas and many different alternatives. We can "try on" these ideas. We can "try on" these roles and see how they may suit us and how they would affect those near to us. However, there is absolutely no obligation to go any further. We can look at and talk about millions of different careers and examine millions of different ideas. This does not mean that we have to do any of them or drop the job that we are currently doing.

The progress that we make will be totally within our control and the steps we take will be the ones that we feel ready to take. If we wish, we can decide not to do anything at all and to stay exactly where we are. However, the whole process is based mainly on looking at the broader picture and showing us that our present position is much, much wider and much more varied than that which we currently see. There are many alternatives out there and there are an infinite number of ways of approaching each of these alternatives. The whole object of these sessions is to impress upon the client that he or she always has the choice in every situation. Probably the most crippling idea that we can have is the sense that we are trapped in a situation and there is nothing that we can do about it.

Many of my clients say to me that they have dependents and financial commitments. That they have no idea why they are undertaking career research because there is absolutely nothing they can do about their situation. In many of these cases, we find out that there are many things that they can do about it. However, in the end, the client may choose not to change their job at all. They may see that they are in the right position already and this is where they choose to be. Their position may not change but their attitude towards it totally changes. In a case where a client does decide to change, this change will be very slow and steady and will always take into account the financial requirements and restraints resulting from emotional and other commitments.

Perhaps one of the most tricky impediments that we have to face is our own cynicism. It asks us, "What if this is all a fairytale?", "What if I raise my hopes just to find out that this is beyond my grasp?" "What if it is all just an empty dream?" We can use the tests described in the following chapters to help us with these decisions but it finally comes down to trusting in ourselves and in the meaning of our lives. We can also see from the examples from other peoples' lives that the answers we seek may have been there all of the time. We may not even need to change our job, we may simply need to change radically our perception of it. In order to see what we need, sometimes we just need to sharpen our perception.

For this reason, this book will not concentrate on encouraging us to change. It simply asks the question, "Could it be that who we are is exactly who we are meant to be?" Could many of our anxieties come from the fact that we are constantly encouraged to change ourselves and "transform our lives"? Is this not saying to us that we are not good enough, that the way we live our lives is not good enough, that we have to change beyond measure to be "acceptable"?

What would we do if we knew that we are perfect just the way we are? That no-one else had the answer for our lives except us? That all we have to do is to appreciate who we already are and to trust that the gifts that are given to us naturally will not only be appreciated by the world, but are badly needed by it. What this book is saying is *"don't change"* – not one little bit! We don't have to "transform our lives". The magic lies in the way our lives already are. We simply need to learn to see and appreciate what we already have. We will be looking at the way we *are* and how valuable our presence is in the world around us.

Could it be that we are born into this time and find ourselves in this place for a reason? Have we been given our own specific, particular gifts to fulfil this reason? These gifts may not relate to just one job, they may relate to many functions. Our life's work spreads out way beyond a mere "job". We need to know that we have these gifts, we need to trust in the knowledge that we have them. As children, we knew that we had special unique talents that set us apart. We never doubted them for one second. We have merely forgotten that they are still there, throughout our passage into adulthood. Other voices which were much louder and stronger gained our ear. We repressed our small voices and did the sensible and safe thing. We took the more travelled, more secure route – it was far less frightening.

We can now listen to these little voices and temper them with our adult wisdom. There may be a gap between our questions and the answers that are given to us. A time which we can use to learn to listen. This is a frightening period as we are asking questions, but it seems as if nothing is happening. This is a time when we are really challenged, to trust in ourselves and in our place in the scheme of things. We can use psychometric tools to help us on our quest. We can avail of the help of counsellors and advisors but perhaps, more importantly, we can trust in our own wisdom and in the messages that this wisdom is giving us now and has always given us through-out our lives. Our simple task now is to learn to listen to this wis-dom.

What if we changed the script and said that work need not be a chore, a curse, but could be one of the many ways in which we can find fulfilment and have fun? What if we all used the intelligence with which we are most comfortable in the workplace? We could then be and feel productive. What if we chose the activity that really moti-vated us? We would then be fascinated by the work we do, we would not be able to wait to learn more and we would be energised instead of drained by our work activities. What if we chose an activity that readily suited our real natures? We could then be more like our real selves at work. We need not hide our personal gifts, we can put them to use. This book would like to touch firstly on issues that stop us taking this route and subsequently at ways which may inspire us to pluck up the courage to get started.

## SUMMARY

- *A career change is not just a change of job but a complete change of lifestyle, affecting not just ourselves but those close to us.*

- *We may feel trapped in our jobs by a sense of commitment, but we learn that we always have alternatives, that the power to choose always lies with us.*

- *A career change allows us to embark on a step-by-step process in which we ask deeper questions such as, "Who am I?" and "Why am I here?"*

- *We can be helped in this process but we learn that the most essential information comes from ourselves. We discover that we already have all of the talents we need.*

- *Our own unique talents are valid and essential to the community at large. It is not a question of changing ourselves but of discovering who we are and who we have always been and of using this essential knowledge of ourselves in everyday life.*

# Two

# "Do I have to be Intelligent to do the Work I Love?"

Perhaps the notion which we allow to limit us most in our choice of career is the notion of intelligence. So many people start their career search by stating, "I know I can never do what I want because I'm just not intelligent enough!" In this chapter, I would like to look at our traditional notions of the concept of intelligence and ask the question, "Do we really understand what we mean by the word 'intelligence'?"

The whole notion of IQ testing came to the fore during World War I in America. It was necessary to recruit a large number of people into the army and it was also necessary to find out at what level these people could be incorporated into the army. Intelligence tests were developed for this purpose by Lewis Terman, a psychologist at Stanford University. The basic aim of these tests was to produce an "Intelligence Quota" or a number which led to an intelligence scale. On this scale, you were determined to have either higher or lower intelligence. Inherent in this result was the notion that one was either born with this intelligence or one was not and, if you were born without it, there was very little that you could do about it.

However, later on in the century the whole notion of intelligence was broadened out and IQ tests were replaced by *Differential Aptitude Tests*, which took as their basis the notion that there was no such thing as one intelligence. It was more true to say that there were several types of intelligence. Therefore, instead of sitting one test, the candidate sat a batch of different tests, each test assessing a different type of intelligence.

In 1983, Howard Gardner in *Frames of Mind*, very much contradicted the IQ view and suggested that instead of one intelligence there were actually multiple types of intelligence. Gardner and his colleagues acknowledged that the possible range of intelligence is actually far more complex than this – particularly, when one takes into account social intelligence, organisational intelligence and such other issues as interpersonal skills.

Unfortunately, however, the vast majority of us are still locked in to the concept of academic intelligence. The main emphases in the traditional school system are on our numerical and verbal skills. If we have not performed well in these two kinds of intelligence, we are given the clear notion that we are not intelligent and will have difficulty learning new skills, no matter what they are. The tragedy of this is that the young person grows into an adult thinking that they are not capable of being intelligent. The picture then is that these two areas of intelligence take precedence over a possibly infinite number of other areas of intelligence.

Gardner and his colleagues would see it as being absolutely impera-tive that, rather than trying to squeeze every child into the mould of the traditional school structure, we should look at the individual child's gifts and talents in as wide a way as possible to identify these natural skills and talents and to make sure that these are encouraged and nurtured in the given educational structure. Therefore, we can say that instead of the child having to adapt to the structure, that the structure actually adapts to the child and that any given talent or intelligence is nurtured and valued.

The very fact that we are alive indicates that we have intelligence. The problem is that the intelligence we may have may not be highly valued by the society in which we live. Maybe when we say that we "lack intelligence", we really mean that we are demonstrating an intelligence that a certain social structure considers unimportant.

The first step we need to take is to broaden out the whole notion of intelligence. As time goes on, more and more aspects of intelligence in the world surrounding us are being discovered. We talk of cosmic intelligence, plant intelligence or the intelligence of minerals such as crystal. We now even consider ourselves differently and talk of the intelligence of our DNA structure or the intelligent functioning of our organs. We have also identified such things as 'social intelligence' which measures our ability to deal with people, to take the lead, to delegate and to be perceptive to their needs. The whole notion of emotional intelligence has been very much brought to the fore by Daniel Coleman. We are beginning to see that there is a world of infinite possibilities in the area of 'human intelligence'.

Concepts such as "intelligence" and "personality" lie so much at the core of the mystery of life that we would be foolish in the extreme to think that we can identify and measure them fully using numerical or rational data. Indeed, no test publishers would ever suggest that they had found the definitive definition of intelligence or that any test was 100 per cent accurate, 100 per cent of the time. What a test can do is to give an indication of possible success in a certain activity when the results of the candidate are compared to the results of a defined group, doing the same activity. This is called the "norm" group.

It is important, therefore, to identify in the adult the natural skills and talents that they possess. When we are using our natural intelligence or the intelligence that comes to us most easily and naturally, we will feel comfortable in the work that we are doing. We will also do our job more productively and competently. When we are more productive, we are more rewarded and when we are more rewarded, we are more satisfied.

In the first two examples, in this chapter, both of the clients fall into identifiable intelligence brackets. However, we find that their areas of highest intelligence are not the ones that they are using in their work places. It is important to note that intelligence can never be looked at in isolation, we also need to consider cultural and emotional environments. The third example, however, is of a client who did not seem to "succeed" in any of the identifiable intelligence aptitude tests. What we can then say is that the tests that we have to hand do not identify the gifts of the individual. In this case, the scores that the individual achieved on every test were extremely low. The challenge in this case is to broaden our scope and broaden our vision, to open our minds to include an infinity of possibilities in the realm of intelligence. If this can be done and areas of natural intelligence nurtured, we can see that in their chosen environment, the individual can be totally competent and successful.

This chapter will suggest that we may well be able to do many jobs but the job that we choose may not suit our strongest aptitudes. Therefore, we may be doing a job quite well but at the same time, we may experience feelings of discomfort, inadequacy and stress. When we are working with our strongest aptitude, the task we have to do generally come to us far more naturally. We generally struggle less and work seems to blend into the "flow" of our lives.

In essence, work begins to feel far less like "work" in the conventional sense of the term. It begins to become an activity in which we can express more of our real selves. We are more constructive in our work and, therefore, receive more positive feedback. Work becomes a place which heightens our sense of self-esteem and strengthens our own sense of ourselves. We come to recognise that we can be productive and effective by being who we are. By being ourselves.

To find a constructive way to feed into our workplace, we need to first stand back from it and ask questions, "Who am I?" and "What do I love to do?" These seemingly simple questions are difficult to answer. It takes time to get a really comprehensive picture. It will be obvious from the following cases that even though the psychometric tests form a valuable starting block, we need to gain a far more comprehensive picture of the individual and the environment in which they find themselves before any choices or decisions can be made.

In the first of these cases the individual was very high in verbal intelligence but was actually working in an environment which valued numerical intelligence. The individual was unaware of this discrepancy and because she could not perform to the same level as her colleagues, she had classed herself as stupid.

## HELEN

Helen had been in her job for fifteen years. She had been aware of a problem for some time but found the possibility of change very frightening. It was her 40th birthday which brought the whole issue to a head for her and brought her to my door. She began to ask herself was she to spend another 25 years doing something that she had never really liked?

> *"I'd love to change my job, the only problem is that I'm not that intelligent, so I don't want to be wasting your time. I haven't got a hope in hell of getting anything better than I have now."*

Helen was distressed and apologetic. Yet, when I looked at her CV, it was like reading about a different person. She had flown through her 'A' levels and then had gone on to take a degree in literature in which she was entirely successful. How could it be that fifteen years later, she was sitting in my office telling me that she was stupid? What did she do in between times?

She explained that her family had not been well off and that her parents suggested that she should go into a "secure" position. Anything to do with literature was just too risky. She was also fearful herself, at that stage, of not getting a job. She was relieved when she found a position as a book-keeper in a financial institution. As she had no training in this area, she accepted a very junior position. Over the years, she became familiar with her job; however, she still had grave doubts about her capacity to actually do it successfully. "Even though I can complete tasks now, I never feel very comfortable. The other people I work with seem to know what they are talking about and speak with conviction. When I say something, it seems to come out differently. People just look at me with an expression which seems to say, "Oh, it's just Helen again.""

Because the issue of intelligence was at the core of the problem for Helen, we decided to concentrate on this for the first few sessions. Helen sat the differential aptitude tests which take into account the fact that there are different types of intelligence. Helen sat a batch of eight tests, each of which measure a different intelligence. It is possible then to measure each intelligence separately and to profile out with which type of intelligence the person is most comfortable and most uncomfortable.

When Helen's profile was compiled, we found that her highest intelligence was verbal reasoning, whereas her numerical reasoning was by far her weakest. In her work, Helen was calling upon her weakest intelligence on a daily basis, while completely ignoring her highest intelligence. All of her work centred around numbers and numerical reasoning.

Helen also gained a high score in abstract reasoning which measures the ability to perceive the relationship between abstract symbols. She admitted to loving the conceptual and the abstract. She enjoyed taking an issue, pulling it apart and coming at it from several different angles. She enjoyed complexity and welcomed as much change and flexibility as possible in the workplace. Her work was, however, totally rational and procedural. Every task was done on a step-by-step basis, based on a pre-determined rationale. Helen was asked to be rational, logical and conscious of detail. Any departure from the procedural was seen to be a mistake and any innovation or self initiative was not appreciated from an employee at Helen's level. '

For years Helen had tried to adapt to the personality and intelligence profile of the firm in which she worked. But none of the skills, which she was trying to perfect, came to her naturally. She tried to follow procedures, and to be conscious of detail but all the while her more adventurous, creative nature was straining to get out. She tried to perfect her number skills, but again her verbal ability fought to be expressed. Helen found that she could not stop talking and discussing issues, looking at different eventualities and engaging people in conversation. Her more numerical, factual colleagues, found this discussion quite unnecessary and because she was also slower with numerical tasks, Helen quickly gained the reputation of being "a lightweight". Over the years, she began to see herself in this light as well.

She thought that if everyone in the firm could do these tasks and she couldn't, then it must be her fault. Her confidence was eroded to the point where she saw herself as being completely stupid and not capable of getting another job.

The process of confidence-building began slowly. Even though she had always dreamed of writing, Helen felt that she lacked the confidence to do so. For the moment, she needed to work in quite a structured job in which she would know what she had to do and would know how to do it. We needed to find a structured job that involved verbal information and had a high level of people contact. We did a great deal of role play and practising for interviews. After three months, Helen heard of a part-time job in a newspaper; the vacancy was for a personal assistant to the assistant editor. It would require dealing with information in a verbal capacity, with work colleagues and customers, and would also involve a good deal of telephone contact. She would be working with people who would be more conceptually-oriented. It would mean a drop of salary and in status, but Helen found that job satisfaction and a boost in confidence was worth this. She applied to the job and was taken on, on a temporary basis.

After six months, she was so good at her job that she was offered it on a permanent basis. We met sometime later and Helen told me that the move she needed to make seemed so simple and so obvious with hindsight, that she wondered why it took her fifteen years to make it. We both agreed that, sometimes, the simplest of moves can seem very difficult and very fearful at the time and that, at some point in our lives, we have all hesitated in making them. Helen added that in her job, she was constantly working on her confidence and raising her sense of self-esteem. She had begun again to entertain the idea of writing in her spare time and she informed me that she felt that, in the near future, she would actually have enough confidence to begin expressing her inner thoughts in written form.

---

In the following example, we see a case which involves exactly the opposite position to that which Helen experienced. In this case, the person involved was very numerical but was actually working in a very verbal and creative area. It will be very obvious from this case that it is impossible to distinguish between objective academic intelligence and traits of personality. We will see that the two are very much intertwined.

Ray was very numerically-oriented but this was also translated in his behaviour by being very organised, detail-conscious and task-oriented. He had difficulty in dealing with groups of people. So, it is true to say that not only was his intelligence unsuitable for the place he worked, but also his whole emotional make-up seemed to be at variance with that of his colleagues. The stress was produced not only by the fact that he was using a weaker intelligence, but also by the fact that his preferred way of behaving was not at one with the general behaviour in the workplace. In other words, Ray was at odds with the work culture.

## RAY

Ray was prompted to reconsider his career because of a simple meeting. He had found out that a meeting of all his colleagues had been held three days earlier and he had not been informed. He felt that this was an indictment by his colleagues and it brought to a head all of the frustrations he had been feeling for quite some time.

During his careers research, Ray realised that, like Helen, his approach to his work differed very much from that of his colleagues. But unlike Helen, Ray was devoted to his job and wanted to stay put. His challenge was to see how much his skills and personality could differ from the general dynamic of his workplace and yet contribute in a very positive way to it while remaining true to himself. As Ray explained:

> *"We would have quite a number of meetings. It's very necessary in the marketing area. But at these meetings, I never really say much and if I do, nobody takes the time to listen. The others are funny and entertaining. They come up with new ideas and make people laugh at the same time. I'm either very quiet or dry and boring."*

When Ray sat the differential aptitude tests, it became clear that he was very high in numerical reasoning. He loved numbers and really enjoyed working with them. From the personality profile, we learned that he liked to work with structure and procedure – he liked the sequence of events to follow rationally. Ray also felt far more comfortable working with facts and objective data than he would if he were asked to rely on intuition. He said that very often he would come home absolutely exhausted. He explained that during the day, he would deal with a large number of people, all asking different questions. Just when he thought he had his day planned, someone would come along with a crisis and all of his careful organisation would go out of the window. He felt that he spent most of his time trying to find his feet and establish some kind of order in a day which seemed to be spinning out of control. When 5.30 pm came, he found that he never got around to doing the tasks he had originally planned and went home feeling very despondent and with a sense of failure.

We felt that it was very necessary to explore, in detail, the dynamic that currently existed in the workplace. More importantly, it was essential that Ray clearly saw that this problem was nothing personal between him and his colleagues, it was simply a clash of two totally different mindsets. By defining, very clearly, the differences in approach adopted by each of these mindsets, it became easier for Ray to understand the present situation and to predict future ones, so that he would not set up any false expectations which may lead to further frustration.

With his love of structures and a rational approach to his work, Ray preferred to work with numbers and his computer. He found that numbers were clear and were either right or wrong. They did not change without his knowing it and, therefore, would allow some type of planning and organisation. If a problem arose with his numerical analysis, it could be solved by logic – Ray knew when he started and he also knew when the problem was fixed. He felt no great urge to communicate on a regular basis with other people. He was far more comfortable working his problem out on his own and getting it absolutely right. Only, at that point, would he be comfortable getting other people involved. If he asked for their involvement before this point, the issue would just get too confused for him. The feedback that he would give to people at the end of the process, would be clear and very concise and usually in numerical or graph form.

When Ray became familiar with his own work patterns, he was then in a position to compare those patterns with those of his colleagues. He saw that they approached their work in a different way. The majority of his colleagues came across as far more inclined towards words. Their thinking processes involved people. They thought as they spoke and it would be imperative for them to have other people around to bounce their ideas against – that way ideas were fresher and more original.

They would be less inclined towards structure and would be more led by the inspiration of the moment. If they were involved in one task and another more exciting or urgent one came along, they would have no trouble at all in dropping it and taking up the new task. In fact, they would thrive on this variety and any strict structure they would find restrictive and boring. They would feed on the interpersonal dynamic and the more that was going on in the office, the more exciting they would find their work. In other words, the very elements that exhausted Ray stimulated his colleagues and the very structures that Ray respected, his colleagues would avoid like the plague. What to do?

Ray's first impulse, when we studied these patterns, was to leave. He felt that it would be impossible to make things work as he seemed to be so different from everybody else. However, on talking with him, it was obvious that Ray really loved the company in which he worked. He worked hard and really cared about its successes and failures. It seemed that in losing Ray the company would be losing a good man. Could it be that Ray's gifts had simply not been recognised by the company and therefore had not been used? How could Ray best use his gifts in such a people-oriented atmosphere?

We decided that the most pressing issue, and the one that was wearing Ray out, was the fact that he had to be constantly available to his work colleagues. In order to allow himself the time to find his feet, even on a short-term basis, we needed to create some space around him that would give him time to think.

I was about to find out that this seemingly sombre man was not only funny when given time to think, he was hilarious. It was Ray who came up with the idea of signs on his desk. The first one read:

*Occupant of this desk vicious – has been known to bite.*

The sign had the effect of making his colleagues wonder and pause a little before approaching. The next session, Ray was in full flight. He had decided he would change the sign each day. The effect was that his colleagues were so intent on seeing what the sign was, that their attention was drawn away from Ray. Howls of laughter used to emanate from my office as we thought of more and more signs. Ray was beginning to enjoy himself – he had become more and more daring. Another sign read:

*Approach with care! Leave a fresh plate of 'Jaffa Cakes' (Ray's favourite biscuits) under occupant's nose. Leave. Come back five minutes later and speak in reverent tones.*

His colleagues, given to the dramatic and the different, were enthralled and entered into the game with gusto. Ray made his point in a funny way and before long, without the aid of signs, people would ask him if they could have a word with him, if he was not too busy. We practised ways of explaining to people very politely and nicely that he was a little busy right now, but would it be convenient for them to see him at _____ (and name a specific time). Before our discussions Ray would not have used these skills. He would have said nothing, silently fumed and completed the particular task with very bad grace. Or he would have just refused gruffly. Because he was gradually able to communicate to his colleagues his preferred way of working and behaving, they understood him a little more and he felt a little more accepted and popular.

Now that Ray had a little more space and time to think, it was time to address the original problem – his contributions at meetings.

Ray would contribute relatively little during meetings. His points would be brief and generally would be outlining the drawbacks and problems associated with proposals which had just been put forward by his colleagues. Consequently, these colleagues found him totally frustrating. They felt that he did not want anything to work. He completely ruined the flow of the meeting and was generally perceived as a wet blanket.

Ray did not see his contributions in this light at all. He felt that by pointing out the problems now, he was saving his colleagues much heartache in the future. While optimism is normally considered a very positive trait, optimists can be very often carried along by their own idea. They are so hopeful of success that they are not willing to pause and look at the practicalities and anticipate possible problems. The pessimist would normally be looked on in a very negative light, because when analysing a situation, they will habitually start by outlining all of the problems and all of the reasons why the idea just proposed could not work. On the other hand, they can also be invaluable trouble-shooters and can anticipate future problems that will save companies vast fortunes and much embarrassment.

So not only did his colleagues find the numerical information Ray was imparting boring, they also felt crushed by his negative approach. Small wonder he was not told about the meeting. Bit-by-bit, Ray began to piece together an approach that could work in his situation. He saw that it was actually a brilliant idea that somebody with his approach formed part of this group. He realised that he provided an objectivity and a counter-balance which the group badly needed. But how was he going to convince the group of this?

Ray decided that he would approach the group with an idea. The ideas which the group proposed would always have to be sent to management for approval. At this stage, there would often be much delay, while management sent memos back and forth looking for clarification. The marketing group found these delays very frustrating. Ray suddenly saw that much of the problem hinged on language. The group was more conceptually and verbally-oriented, management was more numerically and practically-oriented. Ray could act as a bridge. He could be involved at the conceptual stage and then translate the idea into "accountancy speak". It was at this stage that he told his colleagues that he had just started to take an accounting technicians' course at night. The group was interested. The submissions they had to make to management had to be very practical and contained much numerical information. How were they going to achieve this without the group getting bored?

When we completed Ray's aptitude test, we found that he scored very highly in spatial reasoning. How about putting his artistic skills into action? He prepared spreadsheets that were works of art with cartoon characters of some of his team. His colleagues found them hilarious, and this encouraged them to read the information they contained. He also radically transformed his verbal submissions. When talking about ideas, he would always outline the positive aspects first. Instead of using words such as "problems", he would outline them as "issues we might have to look at".

This engaged the attention of his colleagues but it also encouraged Ray to take a slightly more optimistic view of issues himself. He began to recognise his high academic potential and decided to embark on a certified accountancy course. This would establish him as the numerical person within the group but, far more importantly, it would heighten Ray's sense of self-esteem. Not only could he now exist as a data-rational person within the group, he could also have a high qualification in that area.

Having finished his careers research, did Ray still bore his colleagues? Did he ever fail in his efforts to persuade management? Did he ever go home frustrated, tired and fed up with people? Of course he did. Yet his reaction now was somewhat different. He now saw that what was involved in the initial problem was a difference of aptitudes and a difference in preferred ways of behaving in the workplace. He saw that his colleagues were not just trying to annoy him personally. They were just doing the things they did because they felt that this was the best way to do their job. He saw that he could do things differently but instead of this leading to a clash, the group could benefit from the different approaches of each member of the team once they began to respect the differences that lay between them.

---

In the following case study the issue of intelligence was brought even more to the fore for the simple reason that the individual involved did not seem to comply with any of the defined types of intelligence as outlined in the differential aptitude tests. When he took these differential aptitude tests, all of his scores were extremely low. The challenge then was to try to look at intelligence in a totally different way and to establish what other talents, gifts or areas of intelligence this individual possessed which were not being picked up by the aptitude tests. To make this case even more complex, the individual involved was a minor and we also had to deal with the stress of his parents.

As parents, it is only natural that we want the best for our children. We are taught that in order for our children to be successful, they have to attain a certain degree of success in their school exams. Our children are also taught that in order to be successful in exams, they need to be diligent in two types of intelligence – verbal and numerical. Most traditional exams are based upon numerical and verbal intelligence. If our children do not perform well in these areas, they will most likely not do well in exams. If our children do not perform well in exams, it is likely that they will consider themselves "stupid" or lacking in "intelligence". The tragedy is that most young people are oblivious to the fact that there are so many areas of intelligence in which they could shine. Instead of being encouraged to blossom into their natural intelligence, our children are thwarted and withered by this myth of their "lack" of intelligence.

In simple terms then, lack of performance in exams can signal real panic in parents because they interpret this as a forewarning of total lack of success in the future life of their child. On hearing that their child may not be sufficiently motivated in school or may not be performing to the same level as other children, a parent can be extremely distressed. In the vast majority of cases we feel, as parents, personally responsible for the development of our children. If we perceive that there is any deficiency in this area, we tend to blame ourselves. We feel that we have not sufficiently stimulated them or introduced them to a sufficient number of skills when they were younger.

We ask the expert to change our child, to give him or her what the system demands, regardless of whether or not it is good for the child. As parents painfully find out, this can never work in the long term.

We cannot, thankfully, change the true nature of our children. We may try, but we will end up frustrating ourselves and harmfully stunting their natural potential.

Perhaps the most demanding function of a parent is to be able to accept their child exactly the way he or she is. When the so-called challenges arise, it is essential that we are able to sit with our children, to identify their essential gifts and talents and to trust that these individual gifts and talents are exactly what is needed in the world our children inhabit.

However, all the information around us is screaming the contrary. The system tells us that if our children don't follow certain procedures, if they don't succeed in step A, step B and step C, he or she is going to be a failure for the rest of their lives. We are given the impression that the natural gifts of our children are not enough, that they have to be added to in some way. Only those who comply sufficiently with the system can have "successful" lives. It is possibly only when we have children that we really deeply examine the whole notion of success.

Unfortunately, emotions can get even further tangled by parents who interpret their children's success as their own success or conversely their children's failure as their own failure. The challenge to identify our children as individuals in their own right, with individual gifts and talents that are as valuable as anybody else's can seem an enormous task from time-to-time. It is surely difficult to truly value our children's gifts when these gifts may not be valued by the society around us. It is really at that stage that our children need our support and our unwavering trust in their real selves.

The problem is that the real nature of these gifts and talents may not begin to manifest itself for some years. There may be a period in which we doubt ourselves, we doubt our children, we doubt the process. We ask ourselves to consider notions such as, "Maybe society is right." We, unfortunately, compare our children constantly to the children of relatives and neighbours. We try to place our children within the general hierarchy of "success" within our community. When doing this, we very often see our children as lacking or inferior in some way. It is a constant challenge not to see ourselves as failures when we see our children supposedly "failing". It is hard to trust the process when it seems not to be working. In the following example, the child's lack of performance in school signalled a catastrophe for his parents. It went even as far as pre-empting social disgrace and brought up large fears on the parents' part that their son might even be eventually ostracised from the com-munity.

## JAKE

*"I mean for God's sake, not only is he useless in school – he is not even good with his hands!"*

Jake's father paced up and down the room, running his fingers through his hair in a gesture of desperation. He was a self-made man. He had a very large enterprise and got where he was by the use of his considerable academic intelligence and common sense. I had just given him the results of Jake's assessment tests which were all very low. He told me that his two other children were highly successful and that he could not understand what had happened to Jake. I looked at Jake's mother for her reaction. She said that she had no idea where they had gone wrong. I tried to explain that it was certainly not a question of "going wrong" – Jake was a fine young man. But they were still disconsolate.

*"Could we get him to come to you a bit more and could you see if you could do anything with him?"*

I made it quite clear that it was not a question of "doing anything with him", but of merely trying to discover Jake's innate qualities and gifts and to see in what way they could be applied. So started my journey of discovery with Jake.

The first session started and continued in complete silence apart from questions. Jake was a young man of large, strong build, with a very gentle nature. Everything he did was slow and rhythmical as if he was always moving at his own inner pace. He was used to people who spoke to him in a very hurried way, not really listening to what he had said. He had simply lost the habit of having a conversation. I learned that he did converse with his friends so that there must be a topic of conversation that would draw him out. The silence continued. Just as I was about to give all up for lost, I spotted a small emblem on his T-shirt. We both supported the same football team! I shared this information with Jake, but he was sceptical. He tested me on my football knowledge. Did I really love this team or was I only trying to get him to talk? When I answered all of his questions more or less to his satisfaction, Jake relaxed. I was "one of us" and we were on our way!

In the following sessions, after we had discussed all the league positions and possible substitutes for each team, Jake felt ready to broach the subject of himself. I prepared myself to start at the very beginning and to look forward to a number of sessions. What actually happened next left me with my mouth open.

Jake explained slowly and softly to me that he had no intention at all of going to college. His eventual job was only useful to him in that it was a means to an end. His driving force was to find a girl who would love him as much as he would love her. Family was, and would always be, his first concern. The very top of his list of priorities. He would like to have about five children (at this point Jake was eighteen). It would be really important to him that his family would have a nice home so, therefore, he had it all planned out. He planned that he would work near the family home in a local factory. He wished to work on a conveyor belt and nowhere else. Why he wished to do this was that he would have relatively good salary, have a definite, flexible working day and still have plenty of time for his partner and his children. It was very important for him that he would never be promoted as that would only mean that he would have to put more time into his job and less time into his family. Throughout his life, he explained, he had witnessed his father spending every waking hour making money and never having the opportunity of getting to know his children, or really even to enjoy his money. Jake would never let this happen to him or to his family – his life was too short and too precious.

He realised that building a house was expensive, but he had already started saving. He had had a job in a bar since he was sixteen. He knew that he was not very good with his hands, but he had friends who were. He had done them some good turns and later, when the time was right, they could help him with the house. It would not be a big problem as he knew exactly what he wanted. Something simple but cosy and very child-friendly. The small community in which he lived was very important to him. He would like to contribute to it in whatever way he could.

When Jake was finished, I sat flabbergasted. From his slow, quiet, deliberate tone, I knew that this was no pipe dream, thought up on the spur of the moment. This vision of his future had evolved slowly and quietly over many years. I had seldom come across such a depth of clarity and assurance in one so young. Indeed in anyone of any age! He spoke with a quiet conviction that left me in absolutely no doubt but that all of these things would be accomplished. I knew that Jake had no need of my services. I was there more to facilitate his parents. I couldn't wait to tell them of the intelligence and vast wisdom of their son.

> *"You must be joking! No son of mine is ever going to work on a conveyor belt. I would be laughing stock of the place. Do you think his brothers and sisters would want to have anything to do with him if he only worked in a factory?"*

I found it hard to believe that his parents could not see what a gem of a son they had reared. I thought I had not explained the position correctly and tried again. This only made the unfortunate couple even more distraught. His father explained that his son was doing what he himself had tried not to do all of his life. He had worked to gain respect and status for himself and his family. Who would respect or even notice a factory worker? It seemed that the things that his father had worked to achieve all his life, Jake had now turned his back on. It seemed that his father had failed in the task that he had set out to do. I tried to explain that the respect that his son would command would have little to do with his job and everything to do with his wonderful, personal qualities. To this Jake's exasperated father replied:

*"Personal qualities! I can't bear this touchy-feely stuff!
Do you think that you can be a success with just personal
qualities?"*

I asked them if they thought it would be possible for them to trust in
their son's judgement, to encourage him, to give him some time and
see how things turn out. They replied that their son was not capable
of knowing what he wanted. With his level of intelligence, he would
have to be told what to do. He could not be left to decide on his own.
His parents asked me if I could just pick out a sensible job he could
do and tell him to do it. I replied that this would doing Jake a huge
injustice and that I felt that, allowed to follow his own innate wisdom, Jake could be entirely successful. His father left in a rage. Not
only had his worst fears been confirmed, but he had to pay for it!
His mother cried bitterly and again wondered where she had gone
wrong, surely there was something she could have done? All her
other neighbours had achieved it. How was it that her youngest son
just did not make the grade? I tried to reassure her that she must
have been a wonderful mother to produce such a son. But nothing I
could say could convince her that he was not going to turn out to be
a total failure.

I had no further contact with his parents but I kept in contact with
Jake. Two years later he met the woman of his dreams. She loved
children and they started their family straight away. Since he had
taken up a job in the local factory, Jake had had no contact with his
father. His father just could not accept him as a factory worker and
each time he saw him, Jake seemed to remind him of his own failure
in life to produce a successful son. Because of his diligence and
wonderful nature, Jake was as popular with his employers as he was
with his colleagues. He consistently refused promotion but his good
work earned him many bonuses and the work started on their house.

Five years later his father fell ill and had to dispose of his business
interests. He went from being a successful businessman to spending
a large amount of time on his own in his house, in bed. His other
children had high-powered jobs abroad and were not easily accessi-
ble. His wife had problems coping with nursing her husband full-
time and Jake's wife offered to help her. Jake's father was regularly

visited by his two little grandchildren and they became the joy of his new life, so much so, that the front door was always left open for them to come and go. Even though the relationship between father and son was still noticeably strained, these grandchildren seemed to be beginning to heal the wounds of years gone by.

Soon a little football team started in the community on Sunday mornings. The children loved their new coach and the number of fanatical little Manchester United fans in the locality grew dramatically. Jake with his gentle, consistent nature was a constant source of encouragement and motivation for the children. They ran to their football practice with enthusiasm. Even though Jake was quiet in nature and would never be the type to intrude on anybody else's privacy, he was none the less quietly available to anyone in the community who would have need for his services. For example, if his neighbours forgot their keys, Jake was available to climb in a top window to open the front door. Jake had managed to assess his own skills and construct his vision so clearly that he was perfectly comfortable with the life he now lived. He used his innate intelligence consistently to great effect benefiting himself, his family and his community. Now whenever I think of the word "success" I often think of Jake.

---

Would it be possible for us as parents to reconsider our position on the intelligence of our children and on their eventual success? Would it be possible that each child born into our community is given the innate gifts and talents to meet the needs of our community as they arise? The needs of the present may be totally different to the needs of the community 25 years hence. How can we predict what those needs will be? How can we predict how our community, how our country or how our world is going to evolve? If we constantly mould our children into one way of being, into one way of succeeding, one way of thinking, are we not excluding a whole range of gifts and talents and types of intelligence that may be absolutely vital in the years to come?

Would it be possible for us, as parents, as mentors, as the motivators of our children, to stand back and really look at them? To identify their skills and their talents? To encourage our children to use these skills and talents constructively, and finally, and more importantly, to know and to trust that they will be useful in our community and greatly appreciated by it? Would it be possible for us to drop our pre-conceptions about success, about power, about status and to accept that these concepts may be totally turned on their heads and re-evaluated by the future generation?

By not appreciating the innate gifts and talents in our children and by forcing them to accept the same mode of living as we have, we are perhaps stunting the future growth of our race, by placing ourselves constantly in control, arguing, dictating, manipulating, forcing. We may be stunting our children and were definitely frustrating ourselves. Tragically, if we force our children to become what they naturally are not, on the surface, we could have extremely successful children who may be very miserable on a deeper level.

## SUMMARY

- *We think we understand the notion of "intelligence" but this concept is complex and its manifestations are infinite.*

- *The fact that we are alive means that we are intelligent.*

- *When we identify our natural intelligence and use it in our lives and in the workplace, we are most at ease and most productive.*

- *When we work in an area which demands that we use an intelligence with which we are less comfortable, we can experience much stress and unhappiness.*

- *It is not possible to identify all types of intelligence. In which case, we need to broaden our whole notion of intelligence and use other means of assessment.*

- *In order to allow the true nature of our children to blossom, we need to be vigilant to ensure that the system adapts to the child rather than allowing the child to be choked by the system.*

# THREE

# "Is it Possible to do the Work I Love?"

Unfortunately, for many of us, work is something that we feel we have to do. It is a chore, not an enjoyable experience. It requires much duty and responsibility but exceedingly little pleasure and even less choice. In this chapter, we would like to look at the aspect of "interest" and ask the question: is it possible to actually get money for doing the things that we really love to do? In other words, is it possible for us to engage in work in which we are passionately interested, that motivates us and from which we constantly want to learn something new?

I am not suggesting for one minute that every single working day will be blissful. Life is constantly challenging us. However, for some reason, we have the notion that we have to place a separation between the aspects of our lives that really inspire us and the workplace. We tend to interpret work as something that really must be painful, something that must be slogged at. We feel that this is the reason we get paid. I would like to suggest, on the contrary, that work can be something that absorbs and fascinates us. It is something that we can engage in and not notice the time passing. It can be the reason that we hop out of the bed in the morning and look forward to actually going to our workplace.

The work environment is a place where we can learn to express ourselves and continuously learn more about ourselves and about others with whom we work. I am not suggesting that there is one perfect career or one perfect workplace for each person. However, I would suggest that the workplace can be a prime means of a deep sense of self-expression. This again will take the form of a process. We might find that we start our careers in one area and gradually move from one area to another, discovering along the way more and more about ourselves. We may find that, as we change workplaces, we are challenged to discover more talents and skills which we did not think we had and, eventually, to bring the maturity and wisdom of experience and age to our workplace and to use these skills to motivate and inspire the younger members of our team.

A statistic which I once heard at a lecture[1] reinforced my commitment to working in the area of helping people in their careers research. We were informed that the vast majority of heart-attacks in America take place before 9.00 am on a Monday. When the survivors of these heart-attacks were asked what they thought the reason for their illness was, the vast majority of them replied that it was due to stress and unhappiness in the workplace. It turned out that the majority of people were extremely unhappy in the workplace and would have done almost anything to leave, if they had the choice.

Thinking about this statistic depressed me profoundly. I thought about all the hours that each of us spend working. What a large proportion of our lives we dedicate to the world of work. Yet at the end of all this time, are we going to look back and see merely unwillingness, resentment and depression? This vision seemed really tragic to me. I thought that there must be alternatives. Surely, we were not put on this earth to be placed in a prison which is called "work" and to achieve, very, very little when we were in there? Surely, we are not meant to work for people for whom we have no respect and to produce products which we hold in low esteem?

I decided that I would try to create a space in which people could feel free to ask deeper questions about their lives. To look at the broader picture and to consider the many different alternatives which might be available to them.

When we are not quite sure of what we would like to do, in the form of work, the first question that most people ask us is, "Well what would you like to do?" The problem with asking this question, at this stage, is that if we knew that answer, the whole problem would be solved. It is this one, very obvious question, that demands the most attention. The vast majority of my clients feel stupid about the

---

1.   Deepak Chopra at the RDS Dublin in February 1996.

fact that they really do not know what they would like to do. The only thing that they know is what they do not like to do. They think that the least an adult should know is what they would like to do. They say things such as, "Imagine, I am 35 and I still do not know what I want to do!"

We feel that just because we become adults there are things we should know and that, if we do not know them, there is something radically wrong. However, in practice, it is very normal that most of us are unsure. It just happens that at a very young age, we tend to step on a conveyor belt. There seems, at that stage, to be no other option and we merely forget to get off. We are told that at different stages in our lives we need to take different steps and should we not take these steps at this stage, we have missed out. We are "out of the flow", we have somehow "failed". Therefore, at different stages in our lives, we feel quite under pressure to make that decision, to take that step, simply because everybody else seems to be taking it. We are given the message that at the age of eighteen, for example, we should have the wisdom and emotional maturity to be able to make a decision which will remain valid for most of our lives.

In reality, what happens is that at eighteen, we are so busy trying to do well in our exams, that we have little time to think about what we might like to do. Application forms have to be in by a certain date, but we have so much studying to do, that we really cannot see past our final exam. We do not have the time to do any research or to do any type of reflection. We look around desperately for hints on how to make this decision. We talk to adults about what type of jobs they do. We get information on the types of careers which are providing jobs at the moment. We read about industrial trends in the newspaper. We talk to teachers in school who may ask us have we ever thought of such and such an area. But we have no direct experience of any of the areas we are considering. It does not even dawn on us that the answers to our questions may all the time lie inside ourselves. However, this sort of internal reflection takes time and at the age of eighteen, time is something that we feel we do not have.

We come across a career that doesn't sound too bad. We choose it, not because we love it, but because we feel that we have to choose something. We put it down on the form and suddenly we are embarked on a career. At this stage, we say to ourselves that it doesn't really matter, it's temporary anyway. We feel that it is not all that serious. If we do not like it, we are young, we can simply change. We start college, we may have some doubts at this stage but we think that everybody else seems to like this course, so we should give it a chance. At the end of our second year, we might be struggling but we feel that having paid fees and having spent two years studying, we would be rather foolish to give it all up at this stage. We progress to third year.

Now that we have our qualifications, there seems to be very little choice but to go ahead and use them. Aren't we lucky indeed to have our qualifications? We apply for a job and get it. We may be glad in one way. It is nice to have money and to be able to tell our family and neighbours that we are at last doing something useful and taking our place in society. We tell ourselves that this may be really not what we want to do at the moment, but that we will not stay here too long and we will do something in a little while that we will really enjoy. This will be seen as a good stepping stone. The following year, we may be offered promotion and the accompanying salary rise. We would be daft not to take it. And then we meet the person of our dreams. Would it not make sense just to stay a little bit longer and get some money together for a house? An extra little person arrives in our lives and we spend the next four years merely surviving and trying to catch up on some much needed sleep. And then we wake up one fine morning and we are touching 40!

This is the point at which many people ask themselves the question, "I have spent the last twenty years doing things that I do not like. How am I going to spend the next twenty years?"

This little question is in fact a very big one. Any change in career at this stage will have large repercussions for the people close to us. It also requires a profound change in the way we look at our lives. Up to this point, we may have been looking for security or simply for something to do. But now we are asking deeper questions. We are more aware that life does not last forever and we ask ourselves, what do we want to do with it while we have it. Will we just pass the time and wait for retirement or will we choose to use our time as best we can from this present moment onwards?

For most people, the prospect of doing what we love and getting paid for it seems like a fairytale, a totally unrealistic dream. However, I would suggest that doing what we love is the most practical and realistic thing that we could do. Doing what we love will involve using the intelligence with which we are most comfortable. It will mean that we are working in the area which truly stimulates us and will require us to use the personality characteristics with which we are most comfortable. If we are doing all those things, it will necessarily mean that what we will do, we will do well. I would go even further and suggest that the innate gifts and talents that are given to us, are given to us because the community needs us to use them.

Far from this being a completely selfish choice, fulfilling ourselves may be the most selfless thing that we can do. Not only are we, ourselves, happy and an inspiration to those around us, but we are using our gifts and our talents in the most productive way and therefore, benefiting our community far more than if we were simply putting in time, resentfully.

People often feel that if we wanted to do what we most love this involves throwing away all of the things that we have established and abandoning those we love. On the contrary, this process of discovering the activities that we most love, is a slow and gentle process. It can be done step-by-step. We must consider our own needs at every level and also the needs of those close to us. Very often clients consider and experiment with different ideas and activities without ever giving up their full-time jobs. The gradual adoption of a new activity can be done at a time which is most appropriate for all.

Therefore, once again, we engage in a process of discovery. Every project starts with an idea. Most projects start by considering several ideas, hundreds of ideas or even thousands of ideas and filtering these ideas down to the most practical ones. Careers research then is very much the planning stage. The investigation of ideas, the unfolding of dreams and ideals, the expression of hopes and aspirations and the gradual discovery that life can be extremely enjoyable.

It is important for us to bear in mind that our general motivation and interest may go through several different phases during our lives. At the start of our career, we may be in the phase where we wish to establish ourselves in our own eyes and in the eyes of others. At this time, we are very much concerned with constructing an external image of ourselves. We like to give the impression that we are competent, capable and successful. At this stage, we would be very impressed by, for example, being given a company car or going on business trips.

What I have found in my practice is that this phase is temporary. The majority of the clients that I deal with are aged between 33 and 43 years old and by this stage, feel they are moving into a different phase. In this second phase, we are less concerned with what impresses us and more concerned with what fulfils us. We are less concerned with establishing our own personal image and more aware of the wider and the deeper impact of the actions which we undertake in the workplace. We gradually become more in touch with a deeper and more universal belief system. We ask questions such as, "How is the work that I do impacting on the world and the people around me?" and "Is my work making a real difference?"

I have found that the answers to these questions are very much tied in with the way individuals sees themselves in relation to the world around them. At this stage, the individual is less motivated by external stimuli and is more tuned in to internal stimuli. Many of my clients recognise this as a little voice deep down that has been continually prodding them over a period of time. They explain that this voice has even been asking questions in the midst of material success. It asks little questions such as, "Is this really you?" or "Is this really what you want?" They explain that during those periods they probably shut it up and put it back in its box and continued along their merry, successful, material way. However, this little voice was persistent and it was only when the itch got too much that they decided that they just had to scratch it.

We also realise that this inner prompting or this inner vocation is very closely linked to dreams, hopes and aspirations that may have been there since our youth. Many people tell me that when they were very young, they would have mentioned to parents or significant adults that they would love to do a certain activity when they were older. In many cases, they were told that an adult could not do this, that it was totally impractical and that anyway, no-one in their family had ever done this. Wouldn't it be far better if they did such and such a job, that would be much more practical and would earn much more money? For this reason, they were given the message that these inner impulses were somehow not feasible, that they were not being practical and adult by considering these things and that it would be far more pleasing to the people around them to enter on to a different, safer, path.

Many people find that it is not until they are more mature in their working lives, that this inner prompting becomes more audible and more intense. They tend to link up with visions of who they really see themselves as being or who they would really like to see themselves being in the future.

We may start our careers research with no clear vision as to where it is going to lead us. In the next case study, we meet a young woman, who started her career search by trying to solve some practical problems at work. She very much saw the problem as lying with herself and indeed, saw this challenge as being a problem. However, as the sessions progressed Kathy realised that this situation was less linked to her specific workplace but more to her overall dreams and aspirations in her own life and in her life as linked to her work.

## KATHY

> *"I don't think I'm in the right career, I'm not very accurate with figures and I am driving my boss crazy."*

Kathy was an accountant for a large company and basically worked as part of a financial team giving advice to management. For the moment, I took Kathy at her word and we started our assessment session. From the aptitude tests it became clear that Kathy had a very high potential to work with numbers and to work with numerical concepts. From her interest inventory, working with numbers came far above any interest and in the personality profile, she came across as someone who was attentive to detail and highly accurate. All of the assessment results showed that Kathy was ideally suited to her job but the information that she was giving seemed to indicate exactly the opposite. It was clear that the conflict lay elsewhere.

We concentrated on the first aspect – Kathy not being good at her job and making many mistakes. She explained that the atmosphere she worked in was extremely results-oriented, to the point that people felt under so much pressure to produce, that they did not have time to relate to each other. Any kind of talk was considered a waste of time. There also seemed to be much fear and distrust among the employees, as if they were not quite sure, if they did talk, that the content of the conversation would not be brought back to management. Not surprisingly, her colleagues concentrated on their work and did little else. I asked whether this singular lack of people contact at work could be the cause of Kathy's discomfort. However, she explained that, while she did not find this atmosphere the most pleasant, it did not seem to be the primary problem.

We then turned our attention to her boss. On closer inspection it turned out that Kathy's immediate boss was not the problem, being a respectful, efficient and accurate man himself. Kathy received little criticism from him. The real problem was the man at the next level. He had been recently promoted and considered that people would not listen to him or respect him if he did not bellow. On closer examination, Kathy realised that this man was not overly accurate himself, but had the knack of diverting the attention to someone else.

Kathy had informed me that she was considered at work as a person who made many mistakes and as not being very accurate. However, when we discussed this, we realised that many of the so-called "mistakes" she made, could actually be put down to lack of adequate briefing by her boss. We realised that the details of each project she was given were extremely vague and the directions inadequate. The results of her work therefore were necessarily sketchy and inaccurate. We realised also that she had no opportunity to compare her work with that of her colleagues, since there was little communication and much distrust among them. She had to take her boss's word that her work was so inferior.

We thought that we might ask her colleagues some questions about this assertion. Kathy was gradually beginning to take a more positive approach to her work and become more confident about her ability. Things were looking up, but I still had the strong suspicion that we were no nearer Kathy's hesitation about her career. In the next session, I asked Kathy at what jobs other members of her family worked and happily hit the nail on the head. She went into much detail about how wonderful the other members of her family were. They worked in the caring professions. She told me about the long hours they worked, the great good they did and the small amount of money they earned. They were the ones making the real difference. They were the ones at the cutting edge.

She on the other hand, worked in an area that was obsessed with making money. What good was she and her colleagues doing the world in all the time they spent working? The only reason they were working was to make money for themselves. It was self-motivated and greedy. For what reason were they making the money, only to make more money? Kathy explained that this was totally contrary to her childhood dreams and aspirations. When she was small, she envisaged herself as someone who would be very caring and make a huge difference to the world. She was very aware of the suffering that many people had to endure and she felt deeply moved to make a difference about this. She had always seen herself as a nurse, or a social worker. But now she saw herself as merely being a paper pusher. Part of the capitalist world that allowed many millions of people to starve.

Kathy's doubt about her career went even deeper and she began to question herself as a person. She explained that the other members of her family really cared about people, they got involved in their problems and really tried to help. They were warm and welcoming. Kathy, on the other hand, had always been more objective and rational in her reasoning. She would look at the facts and try to progress things from there. This approach would exasperate the other members of the family as they felt that she was not concerned with the "real issues" and did not care. Kathy was cast in the role of being "cold". This casting broke her heart. But she thought deep down that it was true and accurate. She felt that she was destined to work with the materialistic and the financial. Things that were cold and calculating in her mind.

"It's hard being cold and being a woman," Kathy said with deep sadness. I saw that she would be miserable in any job she did until she started to change this negative image of her gifts and talents.

We firstly began to look at the concept of money. For Kathy it was a reprehensible trait in her nature that she was interested in money and how it works. She was looking at how money is used solely in the commercial sector and it really jarred with her world view. I asked Kathy if it would be possible for her to look at money as a tool, as something that would allow her to do things that she thought were really important in life. Gradually, over some time, we drew a picture of what Kathy would like to create. She would use this tool, money, to make life easier for people. She would build medical centres, community centres and more crèches.

When we had a clear picture of what Kathy wanted, we then turned our attention to the people Kathy would employ to run all of these centres. Without her permission in our planning, I placed her family in top positions of responsibility. I placed her mother as matron. I placed her sister as administrator and her brother as financial director. Kathy hesitated for some time, but then voiced small reservations about my choice of staff. She told me that these members of her family may not be the best people for these positions. I asked her why not? Did she not say that the members of her family were so brilliant with people and so caring?

Kathy slowly began to see that there were totally different skills required to run the same centre. While members of her family would be superb at caring for the patients, they would be useless at any type of administration. We then looked in a detailed way at the contribution made by administrative and financial staff. The content of their work may be seen by an outsider as being numerical and factual, but the contribution they made was essential if the centres were to continue. Indeed, if the structure were not first established and carefully maintained, the wonderful work of caring could not continue.

Kathy also began to see the difference in skills. While members of her family were wonderful with people, they did not have the clarity or organisation of thought to plan or maintain an administrative system. Conversely, she with her love of the clear and the practical, would have found that continuous exposure to people on an intensive scale would have worn her out in no time. What was needed was a group of people sharing a multiplicity of skills, working within a structure in which each set of skills was equally respected. It was the combination of many talents which brought the realisation of her dream, with money as the essential ingredient.

Kathy eventually saw that, even though her gifts may not touch people in an intensely personal way, she could still use them to help people make radical changes in their lives. Even though she saw the rationale of the exercises we had done, Kathy said that she needed a little time to integrate these new approaches. She decided that she would stay in her present position for a little while and then possibly consider a course in administration. In the meantime, she would offer to do the books for her favourite charity. Bit-by-bit, Kathy really began to value her gifts and to see that many of the charities that we see today are set up and maintained by people with similar gifts to those she possessed.

Indeed, we learned that Kathy did not need to change her job, or even to change company. What she needed was to see that the essential gifts that she had been given played an intrinsic part in the way the world was run. She did not have to abandon her gifts to realise her deepest personal dreams. They were, in fact, the most essential tools and the foundation stone upon which these dreams could eventually be realised. Kathy learned that she did not have to segregate or alienate any part of herself and that with the constant integration of all the different aspects of herself, her talents could be nurtured and developed to fit in with her compassionate world view.

---

In recent years, we have read about many theories that instructed us to "follow our bliss", to follow our deepest personal instincts, no matter what the consequences. While I would agree that it is very important that we come in contact with our deepest inner desires and motivations, I would also stress that the process is not initiated or maintained by an act of will. We cannot dictate the rhythm of the unfolding of this process nor can we dictate the pace or the progression from one stage to another.

While it is important to establish goals, it is also important to remain extremely flexible and tuned in to our inner radar or that small still voice that we carry inside ourselves. Very often we find that once we take the first step and are intent on following a certain plan or goal, we may be prompted to take a second step which is entirely different. If our will or our ego gets too strongly involved, we might propel ourselves along a road that might not necessarily be harmonious for ourselves and might even be quite destructive for those we love. Therefore, we must be very aware that even though we might be prompted to change our course and to take up a totally different position or job, we must also remain very attuned to the needs of those close to us and to move in a harmonious way so that very little conflict or disruption ensues.

My next client had had an inner prompting for many years and had chosen to ignore it. But suddenly he decided that he could not longer stand his position and started his careers research in a very spirited but rushed way. He was insisting that it would start straight away and he wanted to dictate the pace and the nature of his career progress. From an objective stand point, I gradually saw that it was imperative to slow down this process, in order to verify that the direction that Don has chosen was indeed the correct one for him and the most harmonious one for his family.

## DON

Don chose to come to this country for careers guidance as he felt that he would feel freer to talk when far away from home. He started our first session with a spirited declaration.

*"That's it – I have it. I'm handing in my notice on Monday, now tell me what else I could do?"*

Don informed me from the very start that he had travelled a great distance for this consultation, that it was expensive and that it would be necessary for him to achieve a great deal in one or two sessions. I clarified straight away that I could not dictate the pace or the rhythm of any session nor could I guarantee the outcome of the first or the second or third sessions. I explained that we were both entering into a process and this process would assume its own natural rhythm and unfold in its own way. All we could do is simply attune ourselves to the rhythm and unfolding nature of this process and to respect that this is the way that things should be.

Don had been employed by the naval forces for a number of years. From his aptitude and personality profile, it would seem that he was ideally suited to what he was doing. He explained that he came from a very poor family and when he was accepted for the Navy, there was general jubilation. For many years, at the start of his career, he was deeply involved in his work. He found it continually fascinating to explore different ships and to hold different positions on each of these ships. He was equally fascinated by the amount of travelling he was doing and the countries that he was visiting. Don had noticed that in the Navy, while he really enjoyed dealing with people, he was much more comfortable with them on a one-to-one basis.

Gradually, he realised that the discipline and rigour of the Navy began to be more and more onerous. He felt that the routine that was imposed upon him became more and more difficult to accept. He felt that this disciplined, rigid approach was impeding very much on the way he wished to relate to the people around him. He explained that there was always a certain rigidity and formality in their relationships and that he recently wished to deepen his understanding of people far more than this.

In his current position, Don was dealing with people on an intensive daily basis and he enjoyed this contact very much. He had been due for promotion recently and had been passed over. This was the straw that broke the camel's back. The only thought that had been keeping

Don in his current position was that he had earned a good salary and had prospects for promotion. Now that this promotion seemed to have slipped from his grasp, Don finally realised that the Navy life had not held any attraction for him for a number of years.

Over the last number of years, he had developed an interest in alternative medicine. He had read extensively around the area, and had become friendly with several alternative therapists. He felt a deep resonance with this way of relating to people and felt that becoming involved in this type of work would bring a new richness and integrity to his life.

> *"So it is time to quit, I have decided. I'm going to start studying and take up this job as soon as I can."*

I explained to Don again that what he was involved in was a process and a gradual unfolding. It was imperative that we move at a slower pace in order to give him time to integrate the implications of each step. I added that it would also be very important that his wife was consulted at each stage, so she would not feel frightened by the move and fear for the security of her family. I suggested that if Don would give himself eighteen months, he could then receive a part pension from the Navy and it would also give him time to take steps to make the move easier.

> *"What! You have no idea what torture it is for me to go in there now, everyday. Eighteen months would be like a prison sentence. I don't want the pension, it wouldn't be worth it."*

He explained that it was imperative that he move now. He again said that he did not need a pension, he could work part-time and make money that way. Things would be fine. If he put off what his heart was prompting him to do, he was afraid that he would lose the passion for it and may never do it for the rest of his life. I could see just where Don's fear was coming from. The Navy was such a comfortable and reliable position that he could be easily sucked back into its fold and abandon all dreams of fulfilling his heart's desire. I reassured him that I was as anxious as he was for him to fulfil his dreams and ambitions but that I felt that, if he did rush into this, he would put himself under so much pressure that the project may only materialise for a short time and would have to be abandoned.

Don left this session in and extremely bad mood. He was convinced that I was dashing his dreams and that I had no understanding of what he really wanted to do. He also felt that I was undermining his ability and trapping him in the responsibilities of his family. I got a call from his wife, Kate. Don had come home very depressed saying that he was going ahead anyway. Kate had agreed with my course of action and would have very much liked Don to take things a bit more slowly. Again, Don saw Kate as trying to stunt his future growth and as being someone who was not in tune with him on a deeper level. The resulting disagreement had caused much tension in their marriage.

Don felt that both Kate and I were trying to stop him following his heart. I explained that I was sorry that they were facing so much conflict and asked Kate to ask Don to do just two things. Firstly, to select an osteopath whom he really respects, and explain to him both approaches – the immediate one and the slower and more planned approach. Secondly, to give our sessions one more chance. I would make out a practical, proposed plan of action and go through it with Don, making any changes he wished to make.

Don did contact an osteopath, who gave him much of his valuable time. He explained to Don that this course was extremely demanding and that he would be putting himself under huge pressure by trying to support a family and studying at the same time. He would almost surely have problems passing his exams. He advised Don that, were it possible, it would be extremely helpful for him to have some income coming in while he was studying. This would at least help to ease the financial burden.

I got a phone call requesting that we make another appointment. The plan proposed that Don would take at least twelve to eighteen months to plan his proposed move. During this time, he would study both anatomy and biology in his spare time. Don had not studied biology since 'A' level and had forgotten much of his course. This study would mean that he would have covered much of the first year theoretical side of his osteopathy course. The intervening time would also give him the opportunity to save. We calculated a figure and we found out that, in the intervening time, Don could save the entire fees for the course for two years. The intervening eighteen months would also give him the opportunity to apply for a part pension which would greatly relieve the financial strain of his course of study.

Don also realised that, while he was very excited about heading out on his own and starting a new life, it would also be difficult for him to leave his group of colleagues whom he had come to look upon almost as a family over a number of years. When he actually considered this process, Don did find it a little daunting. He was very close to his friends and began to appreciate an intervening period which would give him the chance to sever his ties slowly and maybe to find a way in which he could still meet with these colleagues in the future. Slowly, Don began to see light at the end of the tunnel.

I have noticed that no matter how much we hate the activity that we are doing, if we can see an end in sight, the job can become much more tolerable. It is really a process of learning to love what we are doing, before we can do what we love. The aspect that we find most depressing is the thought that we are stuck in a position we do not enjoy and that we have no choice but to stay there. Many of my clients come to the decision to stay in their jobs for a short-term period. They may dislike this activity but decide to continue doing this job short-term and to give it their best. As long as they are doing something that fascinates them either in the evenings or at the weekends, they can keep going. We agree to do a certain activity because it is a means of leading us towards something that they love. Depression only sets in when people agree to keep doing that which does not inspire them and do not take the decision to change the situation.

Don saw that the next eighteen months could actually become part of his course and provide the building blocks to make sure that he completed it. Unexpectedly, Don's decisions also gave Kate the freedom to make her own decisions. She had been a nurse and had always wanted to a course in aromatherapy. Because she felt that Don was so unhappy, she had decided that she would say nothing and get him sorted out first. But now that they both had eighteen months, she realised that she could have her course finished in that time, having covered most of the biological side of the course in her nursing training.

Don went back to work with a less heavy heart and started on his biology in the evenings and Kate started her aromatherapy course. I heard from them at the point where Don had just passed his first year exams with flying colours. Kate had just set up a practice at home doing aromatherapy. Even though their family were quite financially challenged, both Don and Kate saw this process as being a thoroughly necessary one in order that they both should feel fulfilled in their lives and in their relationships. In my last telephone conversation with Don, he added:

> *"Wasn't it great that I had the idea not to rush into this course and take my time, Andrée?"*
>
> *"It was Don,"* I replied, *"It certainly was!"*

-----

In the last two sections, we have seen examples of how people took the risk of changing their careers to find a position they would prefer being in and to which they would be more suited. However, what if the activity that we are considering doing is considered by society as one which would not make any money? What if the activity we want to do would not actually earn us a decent living?

This would seem to run totally contrary to the prime objective of traditional work, which is to earn money to keep ourselves and our families alive. In the next case, Mike has chosen to look this very fearful prospect in the face. Actually to take seriously his dreams and desires and impulses, even though at the outset, it seemed to be the most impractical route to take. His fears, particularly at the start about not making any money and leaving his family in difficulties, were very real. This is why we entered into this process very slowly and step-by-step, making sure at all times that sufficient money was coming in to the household to maintain a well balanced family atmosphere.

## MIKE

Mike was the owner of a small retail outlet. It should have made good money but in the previous years it had been losing quite an amount. When Mike came to me, he said that he would have no choice but to sell his business. The only reason the shop was making such heavy losses was that Mike had not the slightest interest in running it. The daily drudge of always having to open at the same time, being responsible for everything for each entire day and having to do the books, proved far too much of a chore for him. He had almost been relieved that it had gone to the wall.

> *"I don't know why I have even come for this session. I know what I want to do, but I can't do it. It's not practical or even possible and there is no way sessions like this are ever going to change that fact."*

I figured that with a start like this, things could only get better. We might as well give it a bash!

Mike explained that ever since he was a child, he had wanted to draw and paint. He would go away by himself and sit by a river and draw. The other members of his family were interested in other disciplines and were successful in their chosen careers. Mike felt that to follow his natural leanings would not be the responsible thing to do and would lead to certain failure. He felt that a far more sensible thing to do would be to get involved in business – it was how other people made their money. The only problem was that it was not the way Mike made money. This was not his first business venture to fail. His other businesses had taken the same route. At this stage he blamed himself – he did not have what it takes. He might as well accept that.

When we discussed the possibility of rethinking his choice of artistic career, Mike was adamant. He had had his chance to take this route when he was younger. He did not take it. He was now married with three young children. He had caused his wife enough stress and heartache. The poor woman never knew where the next penny was coming from. There was no way he was going to indulge his little fantasy at this stage of his life and jeopardise the future of his family even more. I suggested chatting to his wife about even considering the prospect. No, his wife could not be placed in this position.

> *"How could I ever make a living out of art? How could I ever manage to sell any of my paintings?" Mike asked.*

> *"How many do you have to sell?" I replied.*

> *"Oh, none," said Mike. "I haven't done any art work in years."*

I said that it would be difficult to sell paintings, particularly when you haven't got them to sell! Mike got the point.

If we were not looking at the art area, what was the alternative? Mike had heard of a position going in a local factory. It was part-time and paid quite well for the hours he had to work. It would not have been his first choice of activity, but it would pay him far more than he had been earning from his business and it would also allow him to spend far more time with his children than he had been doing recently.

Mike's business was sold and he applied for the job. However, the position did not come through as quickly as he anticipated. Mike had time to kill. I asked whether he would contemplate doing some drawing. Not to sell, but just for himself. Would he be able to draw just for the love of drawing as he used to do as a child and not have any concern about making money out of it? He would not have to dedicate his whole time to it, just a few hours every day.

> *"What if what I produce is rubbish? What if I have lost any gift that I had before? I don't think I ever had any talent in the first place, maybe I'm fooling myself and this is just a pipe dream?" Mike said nervously.*

> *"So what?" I replied. "We are not looking to make any money out of it. Don't concentrate on the end product, just enjoy the process!"*

Mike went home and sometime later, I received a rather bulky package in the post. I opened the careful wrapping to discover two beautiful drawings framed and signed by Mike. It was one of the most touching presents I have ever received. Mike's drawings now occupy pride of place on the wall in my office. I refer to them regularly. When clients tell me, "I'd never be able do that." I reply, "Really? The guy who did these drawings persuaded me he could not draw." The response from my clients is always, "You're not serious?" For me, an even more valuable outcome of these sessions, was the letter I received from Mike's wife sometime later. I keep it in a safe place and refer to it whenever I need reassurance. In it she said that the atmosphere of the household was so much brighter and lighter, she added:

> *"I'm enjoying all the new shades of this man I met abroad, so many centuries ago. More like the chap then than the blank man who'd appeared there for a while. So the floors get covered in "earthquakes" and sketches. I'm watching with relief and joy as this creative person unfolds!"*

I decided that I would have to include this case in my book and rang Mike for his permission. It was at least a year later and I had fears that perhaps this new creative man had been swallowed up by the pressures of living or the demands of the workplace. However, the person that answered the phone was as happy as ever. He assured me that not only was he drawing and painting but that he had started to experiment with several different processes. Not only was he doing his art in his spare time, but at Christmas time the management of the factory he worked in wanted to decorate the walls of the restaurant.

Our Mike took to this task with gusto and was complimented by all of his colleagues for the wonderful work that he produced. Not only that, but the company subsequently decided to add on a large extension to the factory. This extension consisted of some long and very bare corridors. Mike approached the company and suggested that, instead of paying for professional pieces of art to decorate the walls of the corridor, perhaps they could run a competition for their very extensive work force and select the winning paintings from this competition to decorate the corridors. Mike saw this as a way of encouraging creativity among the workforce in general. Mike's interest was beginning to make some money and his passion and enthusiasm for art was beginning to rub off on his colleagues in the workplace.

## SUMMARY

- *The workplace can be the prime means of self-development and self-fulfilment.*

- *We can consider stepping off any career conveyor-belt we happen to be on at any point in our lives.*

- *Doing what we love is the most realistic and productive thing we can do. We are at our most productive and are most happy when we are stimulated and motivated. We are also using our talents to maximum benefit within our community.*

- *Doing what we love taps into the dreams of our youth, to our sense of "mission" and "vocation". We try to express through our work the very essence of who we are.*

- *While we can attempt to clarify our goal, we cannot control all of the elements in our lives.*

- *We need to trust in the natural progression of time and to rely more on our innate wisdom.*

- *What may seem to be a very impractical interest initially may throughout the process gather its own momentum and create its own validity.*

- *It is possible to be happy at work and to be paid for the pleasure of doing it.*

Four

# The Dynamics of Success and Failure

If we look deep in our hearts, the majority of us want to be successful in our work and to be seen as successful by our significant others.
When we look at the concept of being "successful", it seems such an
easy idea to understand. However, when we look at it more closely,
we realise that the definitions of success are actually infinite. This
difficulty with the definition of success can cause many problems.
Basically, what can be a huge success for one person, can be a complete failure for another. I have found over the years as a careers
consultant, that the desire to be seen as successful is a huge motivating factor for the majority of people. We will work extremely hard to
achieve this image of success. However, what I have also noticed is
that there can be a huge discrepancy between how we view ourselves in the area of success and how we are viewed by others.

In order to be successful, we set ourselves goals. These goals, particularly at the start of our careers, are normally of a material nature.
We tell ourselves that once we gain any type of employment with a
large company, we will be seen by others as being successful. However, once we start working with this company, we realise that there
are many different levels within it. There is the basic level at which
we have started, but then there are several other steps within the
hierarchy. Suddenly, our perception of success changes. We quite
voluntarily move the goal posts. We start to consider our current
position in a less successful light. Success we now interpret as gaining that promotion. We work very hard to do this and to make an
impression on the authorities and then, if we are lucky, after a certain
time we gain this promotion.

For a certain period of time we feel successful. However, we then
notice that people of our own age or perhaps only slightly older are
actually at a higher level. Again, the goal posts shift. Our internal

vision of ourselves as being successful again changes. Success for us now lies at the next level. This process can continue indefinitely. We may find ourselves caught on a conveyor belt of feeling inadequate and the only way to feel more adequate is to gain that next promotion. However, in the present moment, it is this feeling of inadequacy that mainly prevails.

Not only do we feel we must be successful internally, this image must also be displayed externally. At the start of our career, the image of success may be buying a car. Once we manage to do that, we feel powerful, we feel mobile, we feel independent, we feel successful. Then we start driving. We notice that the majority of people on the road are actually driving bigger cars. We may find that we have only owned our car for a very short period of time when we start planning to buy our next one. The next one will be bigger, more expensive and will create an even better image.

We then plan to buy a house. At the start, we are so grateful to own any house and to be able to give any address. However, we may find that we occupy this house for only a relatively short period before we start looking at other houses, bigger houses in finer neighbourhoods. The house that so recently enthralled and excited us is now looking rather shoddy. All in all, we find that we enjoy our car, our house, our present position at work for such a short period before the "shoulds" set in. "I should be promoted to the next level", "I should save and be able to afford a bigger car", "I should be able to move house within two years." In all of these areas, the present moment is inadequate and the only way that this will be resolved is to gain more in the future.

What I have found in my practice is that those who visit me would be viewed as being extremely successful by other people. When we start talking, however, it often emerges that the image of success is only a veneer which masks deep feelings of inadequacy. We are generally so focused on what we have not got in the present and on what we should have in the future that we do not see at all what we actually have in the present. The tragedy is that very often we do not give ourselves the opportunity to enjoy what we have right now and to maximise and capitalise on the gifts and the talents we can use right now because we have our eye on the ball, way in the future. In the future, things will be better. In the future, I will be more successful. In the future, I will be able to attain the image that I need to portray myself to others as being successful.

It may be obvious to people around us that we are stuck in a vicious circle and that we need to step back and analyse our present situation. Sometimes, career sessions can offer us some time out. They can offer us the opportunity to step back and not observe the circumstances themselves but the dynamic that is driving them. We may discover that what is driving us is not a lack of material possession but really a lack of self-worth. This may come from the fact that we have never identified our strong points. We have never stepped back and really appreciated the value of what we do, not from an external perspective but more from an internal, personal and interpersonal point of view. Perhaps this stems from the fact that we basically see the contribution that we make to the work place and to society as being essentially meaningless in itself and that it only becomes meaningful when it is validated by others and by society at large.

If there is no external reward for our work then surely our work must not be as important or as meaningful as work which is highly rewarded. In this way, we link the meaningfulness of our work with the reward that follows it. Therefore, the bigger the reward, the more meaningful is the work that I do, and in turn, the more meaningful is the life that I live.

In this chapter, I would like to propose that any action that we take is meaningful. That all of our lives are meaningful. The very fact that we are alive and that we are here is meaningful. I would like to propose that the meaning and the reward for our work does not necessarily have to come from an external source. We can begin to validate every single action that we do in the present. We can see meaning in it for ourselves and even if we do not see meaning in it in the present, we can learn to realise that that meaning will somehow fit in with the overall jigsaw of things in the future.

I have often been struck by the fact that at funerals of people I have loved, those close to the deceased always outline the little things they have done during their lives. They never make a list of the cars that they have owned, or the houses in which they have lived or the money they have made. What appears most meaningful, in that most telling of times, are the little works that they have done. Particularly those works that nobody else ever knew about. These little underground actions of goodness that may have been seen by very few people but may have been felt by a great many. All in all, we can never tell the impact of our actions. We can never measure the value and the meaning of our work. The external reward that we get from it will always be only the tip of the iceberg, no matter how great that reward will be in monetary terms. We need to become aware of the greater scheme of things. To begin to see what the wider impact of our actions may be. In this way, perhaps, we can just begin to start appreciating what is happening right here, right now.

I had an experience which brought this very clearly to mind for me. I was counselling in a school for quite a while and had regular contact with many of my students. I worked very hard in this position but often wondered whether my work was actually achieving anything. I often noticed myself trying to control it and trying to establish what results I was getting. After about two years, I was in town in my favourite cafe and was just about to sit down and have a cup of coffee when I met a former student of mine. She had left school a year earlier and I had not met her since.

I always felt it was a privilege to know this girl. She had such a wonderful, kind, warm nature. She was of a sunny, caring disposition. We began to talk and catch up on the intervening period. She asked me whether I was still involved in the school. I was. She asked me how I felt about my job. I told her that I really enjoyed it but that, sometimes, it was very hard to estimate whether the work I did made any difference at all. She looked at me for a while and said, "But don't you see that it's not the work that you do that is important, it's the fact that you are there." I told her that I didn't quite understand what she meant.

She went on to explain to me that she was doing her mock examinations for her Leaving Certificate in the month of February. Her weakest subject was Maths. She had just received her first Maths paper and had read down through the questions and felt that she couldn't answer any one of them. She said she had felt that old familiar feeling of despair and uselessness, and of being entirely and totally inadequate. She said that at that moment it dawned on her clearly that she would not get the points that she required to do a course at college about which she was passionate. She reasoned that if she was not able to do this course she would not, therefore, be able to embark on the career that was so important to her. What was the point in continuing? During that year she had had one or two thoughts of killing herself but now it came very clearly to her that there really wasn't any other option.

She said that she sat quite relieved and very calm and was rationally deliberating how she was going to do it. Suddenly, apparently, the door flew open and I came rushing into the examination hall. She told me that not only was I carrying books but that I was also carrying a bag of nappies and a spare bottle for my baby. I came dashing up to the woman who was supervising in the hall, gave her a message and walked very quickly down through the examination hall which was filled with about 200 girls. Apparently, I passed by her desk and she said that I gave her a bright smile and a wink and flew off. She said that she had no idea where I was going, but the fact that I was there in the room for 30 seconds made all of the difference to her. She said that she had always noticed that I was very cheery and happy. In that moment, she decided that if I could cope with my life she could also deal with hers. She set about tackling her maths exam.

I looked at this girl, totally aghast. She had always seemed to me to be one of the most balanced girls I had ever met. The thought of this girl even contemplating suicide seemed to be absolutely ludicrous to me. What really shocked me was that I had absolutely no recollection, whatsoever, of that day. I was struck with awe by the fact that a completely unconscious gesture on my part could have had such huge repercussions on someone else. I realised that the timing of my entrance and departure that day had absolutely nothing to do with me and that there was no way in which I could have known of the dilemma which was taking place in her life. Indeed, had I not met this girl that day, I would never have known of the implications of that gesture. It also struck me that I was putting such an amount of effort into my work, trying to make it successful, when it was really my natural gestures, of which I was totally unaware, which were ensuring the biggest success.

With my clients, one of the main objectives, particularly in initial sessions, would be to become more fully aware of the actual impact of the work that they are doing at the moment and only when they are fully aware of this would they move on and try to plan any future actions. Very often, I find, that once people become more aware and value more the contribution that we are making in the present, we can then clarify our plans for the future. The following three case studies will examine different aspects of the success and failure dynamic. The first case study is of a woman who was working within the home and wished to work outside it. The second case study is of a woman who was working with a small company in what she saw as a very insignificant position. The third case study is of a man who was working in management within a very powerful organisation but felt a failure because he had not gained a recent promotion.

## ELLA

Ella had been working within her home for fifteen years. She had raised four children of whom she was very proud. Her children, however, were now grown up. The two younger children were still living with her but they were teenagers and she felt that they no longer needed her continued presence in the house. She admitted that she always felt that her work within the home was not viewed as being terribly important. However, she had stayed and done it willingly for the sake of her children. She had never really considered it as "work".

She completed her tasks as they arose, but always considered that people who worked outside the home were doing the "real work". She felt that now her chance had finally come. The children were grown up, there was less work to be done in the house and she could achieve her dream. She explained that she would love to have some place to go in the morning. She watched other women in her estate coming busily out their front doors early in the morning, dressed in business suits and carrying briefcases. They hopped into their cars and drove purposefully down her road. She felt that they were so lucky that they had some place to go. They really looked as if they knew what their lives were all about and knew where they were going.

She, on the other hand, was the person who stayed behind. Life either came to her or it didn't. She felt that she had little control over events and was basically at the beck and call of the people around her. She wanted ultimately, to have more control over her life and to seem to others as if she had more control over her life. She wanted to buy her suits and carry her briefcase and pop into her car and drive down the road with great purpose, but felt that at 50, she had left it too late. "What type of job can a woman get when she is 50?" she asked quietly. I answered that it depends on what she wants. I asked Ella did she have any notion where she would like to go after driving purposefully down the road. She admitted that she had never really taken her train of thought that far!

We discussed for some time whether she would feel comfortable about leaving her house and entering the workplace. Yes, she was absolutely sure she would. She had had enough of the atmosphere of her home and she was now ready to leave, spread her wings and discover herself in a totally different way.

Having established this, we embarked on the process of assessment. What did Ella love to do? What really motivated her? What aspects of her personality did she enjoy using and with what type of intelligence was she most comfortable? She was a very elegant woman with exquisite taste and had a very fine sense of colour. She explained that she had always loved clothes and texture and colour. We discovered that she had very well-developed people skills, with a gentle but persuasive nature. She could be very encouraging and motivating to others. Gradually, the picture of a sales person in a clothes shop emerged. Ella was very excited by this prospect.

We gradually began to build up a picture of the clothes shop in which she would really love to work. It took her quite a while to even muster up the courage to tell me the name of the shop in which she wanted to work. It was a very exclusive boutique. She said, "I feel really stupid about even thinking about wanting to work in this shop. I have no experience, I would be far too old and," she continued, "they would want someone very young and intelligent and experienced in that shop." I answered that, in reality, we had no idea what type of people that they would like to employ and, even if they had been employing young people up to this point, we still could not predict whether or not they would wish to employ Ella. After much deliberation, we finally drafted out a letter of application and Ella sent it to the shop of her choice with much fear and trepidation.

She rang me up soon after absolutely delirious on the phone. Not only had the shop received her letter, but they had called her for interview. "Oh my God, what have I done," groaned Ella. "I'm going to make a complete idiot of myself, I have never done an interview in my life. Once they meet me and see me, they will realise that they have made a terrible mistake." Finally, she calmed down and we agreed to meet to go over interview techniques. Ella was so nervous that it was difficult for her to be herself. I suggested that she just go in and do the interview as naturally as she could, and if the job was meant to be for her, then she would get it.

The following week she arrived at her interview, a nervous wreck. She met two very kind but very crisp and business-like people. They interviewed her for 30 minutes and offered her the job straight away. Ella was so bewildered and excited that she could only mumble her acceptance. She rang me in a state of delirium and we met for a celebratory coffee. The job was due to start the following week. Ella landed the job of her dreams and she was the last person who thought she could ever do it.

Two weeks passed and one morning I received a phone call from a very distraught and worried Ella. She had started her job and was very successful in it but had suddenly realised that this was not the place for her. Now that she had taken her part in the world of work, she realised that this was not where she wanted to be. She found the strict routine of having to work certain hours everyday to be very restricting. She realised that she could no longer do the things that were terribly important to her. She could no longer just be around for her family. It was now impossible to arrange a last-minute coffee meeting with one of her friends. More importantly, she found that she could no longer get involved in community activities that used to give her a great deal of satisfaction.

She explained that in the past she would regularly drop in to elderly neighbours to see how they were getting on, to see if they needed any extra cooking or just to chat. These activities beforehand had seemed so mundane, so ordinary, so unimportant to her. But now that she could no longer do them, she realised just what an important place they occupied her in life. "I know I have only been here two weeks, but I now want to resign, are you going to absolutely kill me?" I explained to Ella that, on the contrary, this decision of hers was not a failure, but a major success.

Up to this point, Ella had very much resented her position at home. She had not appreciated the fact that, because her husband earned a good salary, she was then free to make many other decisions that she couldn't have normally made. She felt resentful of the fact that because of her children, she had to stay at home and do certain work. She had created in her head a fantasy world of work, where people left their homes and went out and found utter fulfilment in the workplace. Now having achieved her dreams and actually gone out and done the exact thing she wanted to do, Ella suddenly realised that her fulfilment did not lie there. It lay in fact in the place that she had left. Now the activities that she had cast aside as being not important suddenly became the ones she longed to do.

At last, Ella plucked up the courage and informed her employers that she was leaving. They were quite upset having just gone through the procedure of hiring her. However, when Ella explained her position they completely understood. Ella returned home. However, home was now a totally different place for her. It was the place where she chose to be. The activities that she was now doing were ones that she was choosing to do. Gone was the obligation and the tediousness and these were replaced with a sense of gratefulness and appreciation.

Ella also realised that there were personal gifts and attributes that she possessed that she had not developed previously in her home. In her interest inventory, she had displayed a strong interest in the area of visual arts. She had also achieved a high score in her 3-dimensional thinking. At last, she began to give herself permission to potter around creatively in her home. Bit-by-bit, she began to realise that her fine sense of colour and taste could be materialised in her home and, not only could it be done in her home, but people outside her home admired her taste and were willing to pay her for her services. Ella began to entertain the idea of giving creative courses. These she has not yet done, but her home suddenly became the springboard of many opportunities, instead of four walls that had previously trapped her. She could be herself in her home and she could develop herself from it.

She also began to realise that in meeting her friends and casually dropping in on neighbours, she was doing an invaluable community service. She began to appreciate the number of friends that she helped with a listening, understanding ear and kind words of advice. She saw that these words weren't casually thrown about but were actually having a positive effect on the lives of those she knew. She wasn't gaining any external reward for these services. She wasn't getting paid for visiting her neighbours or advising her friends, but she was beginning to build up a vast amount of self-esteem for herself. She began to value personally her own actions and to appreciate the results that ensued, no matter how small or seemingly inconsequential they seemed to others.

## RUTH

Sometimes, even though we have been working in a certain workplace for many years and have gained financial rewards, we can still totally underestimate and under-appreciate the job that we do. Even though we are given money at the end of month which is commensurate with success, we still feel in some way that we are getting paid for doing nothing. Ruth was working as a secretary in an insurance company. She explained that she had been working there for fifteen years and that she was fed up doing work that was totally unimportant. She wanted to make a difference in the world.

*"It is so repetitive. I never do anything but just type letters and more letters. Even these letters are so boring and repetitive. How can one ever get excited about insurance?"*

She explained that she just had to get out. It was a big world out there and it was time that Ruth made a difference. For fifteen years her work had, in her opinion, made absolutely no difference at all. When we did her personality profile, it turned out that Ruth was quite a people person. She had a high level of empathy and she explained that it was important that if she was going to dedicate eight hours of her day to the workplace, she would need to know that the work she was doing was having a positive effect on other peoples lives.

*"You could never have much of an effect on other people in an insurance company."*

However, she was worried, she felt trapped. She had passed her Leaving Certificate but had never done any further training. All she felt she was qualified for was clerical work. She didn't particularly want to, but she was prepared to stay in the clerical area, if she felt that what she was typing was just a little bit more relevant.

I began to ask Ruth in more detail exactly what her job did entail. "I simply type letters," she replied. "What type of letters?" I asked. "Boring ones," she replied. After much prodding, we both realised that her letters were in fact far from boring. I asked her "What would happen to people if these letters weren't written?" She said that people then would not get information that they needed to know. And if they didn't get this information, what would happen then? "They would be totally confused," she explained.

It turned out that the majority of Ruth's letters were in reply to claims that people had filed on personal accidents. These letters would explain to the person exactly what procedures they should follow and what the consequences of their actions would be. Ruth explained that very often her boss would dictate her letters but as she was typing, she would realise that the information given wasn't sufficiently clear. Her boss had a tendency of falling into insurance jargon and

Ruth was always very vigilant about translating this for the client. On many occasions, she would take the letter back to her boss and explain the section that was unclear and ask for his permission to change the letter. On almost every occasion, this permission was given.

Ruth had omitted to tell me that she would also answer the phone to these clients and, if there were any queries on the letter and her boss was busy, she would answer questions in very simple terms and many times to the great satisfaction of the client. On some occasions, they would have to call to the office to see her boss and, if they were kept waiting, Ruth would offer them a cup of tea or coffee. It became apparent that, while her boss was extremely efficient and good at his job, Ruth was more the public relations person. While her boss solved the problems, Ruth related to his clients. "So, I can talk to people, what is the good of that? Can't everyone do that?" asked Ruth.

We then began to look at a scenario where there wasn't anyone in the office with the skills to relate to the clients either by letter, on the phone or in person. Even Ruth had to admit, after a time, that perhaps they would lose many of their clients and, even if they kept their clients, these people would very often wander around in a state of confusion. In further sessions, Ruth began to appreciate the fact that, each time a client contacted her company, they were normally very distressed and under pressure. She had the natural skill to listen calmly, to speak calmly and to reassure the clients that if their question was not answered straight away, it would be done in the very near future. She also had the skill to calm clients who were panicking about pending court cases.

Slowly, Ruth began to appreciate the far-reaching effects of her work. She suggested to her boss that they make the reception area far more comfortable. She acquired some cosy chairs and took it upon herself always to have fresh flowers in this room. Every client was offered a cup of tea or coffee and she always made sure that there were current magazines available for them to read. As she became more confident, she negotiated with her boss that she would play the role of receptionist and that he would employ a more junior secretary to do the typing. Ruth was still very vigilant about the letters that went out, making sure that they were clear and precise. But now she had the possibility of being more free to actually meet and relate to people, to talk with them both in person and on the phone, to give them the time they needed and not to feel pressurised to type the next letter. The atmosphere in the office changed tangibly. Even her boss felt more relaxed in the new ambience.

In the final session, Ruth was at the point where she was contemplating doing a part-time course in counselling. She reasoned that she would thereby gain invaluable information both for herself and for her clients. If she felt more confident about her people skills, she felt that she could keep calmer in stressful situations.

From these sessions, Ruth realised that, far from needing to leave her work, she actually needed to engage in it more fully. She needed to bring more of her real self to her work, to offer more of her warm, genuine nature and, in this giving, she would then do her job in a far more complete way and get a far greater sense of fulfilment from it. The world of insurance now seemed to Ruth to offer a very worthwhile service to her clients and her added input ensured that a potentially highly stressful experience may be rendered into one with which her clients felt more able to cope.

Ruth realised that she had made many value judgements about the insurance industry. She had bought into the public perception of it and had never tried to make it her own. Now that she had stepped outside the public perception and asked the question whether she may take her own place in it, it became a totally different industry for her. The job didn't change, but Ruth's perception of it changed dramatically and, in so changing, she changed the atmosphere for everyone around her.

---

## JAMES

James had been working for a large corporation for the last twenty years. He had entered it directly from school and had progressed to a managerial position. He came to me, initially, feeling very sad and resentful. He felt that the corporation was not sufficiently aware of his skills and talents and that these were in no way being rewarded in the workplace. He explained bitterly about many of his colleagues who had passed him by. His biggest problem was that many of the groups with which he worked were comprised of people who were considerably younger than him. He saw himself basically as being the "daddy" of many of these groups.

One of his first statements was, "At my age, I shouldn't be where I am. I should be in a far higher position in the company. All of my work colleagues have attained this and all of my friends with whom I socialise outside are in much higher management positions." I asked him what position would he specifically like to occupy. He replied that the actual position was not important, what counted was the status that was attached that was. James had identified the title of his work position as being his first priority. He had simply come to me to give him the skills to attain his goal.

> *"I know there must be tricks to this," he said. "The others must have learnt them. I just want you to give me some pointers as to how I can be more successful at interviews and get what I want."*

I explained to James from the outset that while we can prepare for interviews and look at different techniques, which can be used, the one ingredient that will impress an interviewer is integrity. The good interviewer will smell at 100 paces an interviewee who is acting and merely going through the motions. If the skills and aptitudes which are being professed by the interviewee do not form an integral part of that person's personality, the whole effect is false and forced. I explained clearly to James that it was not a question of tricks, it was more a question of bringing out the innate gifts and talents which he already had within himself. James was initially rather dubious but decided that he would go ahead with his sessions in any case.

When James did his interest inventory, there was no specific career that seemed to fire him or make him feel impassioned. This was quite an unusual result and I asked James about it in a subsequent discussion. He explained that work never really inspired him. That he was simply willing to do what his employers wanted him to do as long as he gained the title and position that he wanted. I asked him where he wished to do a little bit more research in to what might inspire him personally. He replied that he didn't really see any point in doing this, at that moment, because he had already identified his goal. I questioned him as to whether that goal was really valid for him and he replied that that was what he wanted to work towards, and that is what he intended to do.

We moved on to the personality profile and the results of this were even more interesting. When I initially met James, he came across as being a very brisk and efficient business man with a gruff and aggressive tone of voice. He gave the impression that he would not suffer fools gladly, that his time was valuable and that one would want to get to the point fairly fast. In the personality profile, however, James seemed to come across as somebody totally different. He described himself as somebody who was very gentle, who avoided aggressive and confrontational situations at all times, who was interested in and caring and tolerant of people and who had no real desire to take the lead and manage. It must be borne in mind that this was a self report profile, so this is how James, in the profile, saw himself.

When he looked at the results, he was quite shocked. He first of all tried to find a flaw with the system and then suggested that he had misinterpreted some of the questions. We went back to basics and checked the questionnaire from the start, yet, we still came up with the same result. James was devastated. He explained to me that the profile he had before him was the profile of a failure. He asked:

> *"How could I change the answers to the questions to make me look like someone who would be more management material?"*

I suggested to him that perhaps instead at looking at who he would like to be, could we perhaps look at who he was, right now, right at this present moment. He explained that he rarely relaxed at work. He said that he couldn't be himself. He couldn't be the normal, relaxed, gentle James. "Nobody would take me seriously in my working environment, if I were." I asked him if he was always acting or if there were times when he actually allowed himself to relax. He explained that there were times when he allowed himself to be the real James and this occurred when he was dealing with people who were younger than he was.

When he talked about his younger team members, he portrayed a real, deep, sense of caring about their present and future welfare. It turned out that he had spent many extra hours after work and during lunchtimes listening to their problems, listening to their future plans and guiding them as to what steps to take in their future careers. His help and encouragement was of a very gentle nature and he was always very diplomatic in his approach.

> *"No-one ever knows I do this," he explained. "These young people wouldn't like others to know that they had to come to an older member for advice, so you have to be very careful and discreet."*

I asked him was he successful at what he did.

> *"Yes," he replied. "It seems to be very helpful to these young people and I find that more and more of them approach me".*

> *"So, would you consider yourself a success"? I asked.*

> *"No," he replied. "This type of thing couldn't really be called work, could it? It's not very important, it's not part of the workplace and in fact, if my colleagues found out that I was doing this kind of thing, they would just see it as being time wasting, inconsequential and would point out that we should be discussing client accounts."*

I asked him about the possibility of letting more people in his workplace know of the role he played.

> *"Absolutely impossible," he said. "If anybody knew that I was so people-oriented and took this non-directional approach, I would never be considered as management material?"*

I tried to explain to James that the role he was playing was the very essence of management.

> *"Indeed it is not," he replied gruffly. "You have to get out there. You have to put your stamp on the world. You need to let them know who is the boss. You need to let your superiors know that you can cope with things, that you can make hard and fast decisions and stand by them. If I told anybody about this, I would just be seen as a wimp. So how can I change this profile to make me look more like management material."*

I explained to James that it was not simply a matter of changing the actual profile because the profile reflected himself. It was a question of changing himself from the inside out and making this huge compromise to merely gain a title.

> *"I'm willing to do it," he replied.*

On further examination of the profile, it came to light that the type of management position that James was targeting would have been extremely stressful for him. Not only would he have to totally change his personality to fit the image he was describing but also his verbal and numerical aptitudes did not seem to be sufficient to meet the requirements of that particular job. He insisted that he could improve, that he could change. We had a long discussion about the negative effects of extreme stress in the workplace. I shared with James my fear about him not being able to do this job, and to change his personality, on a long-term basis. He didn't seem to care. "Just show me how to do it," he said.

I had to again explain to James that I had no tricks, no magic wand, no crystal ball. The only thing that I could do is to reflect back to him exactly how he was. I tried to tell him that he had far more special and precious gifts to give the world than merely to be the type of manager he wanted to be. That this choice he was making was very much a secondary choice that could do damage to himself and to his family. He had explained to me initially that he was under so much stress at work, that he used to bring a lot of his fear and frustration home. This was having very adverse effects on his family. I asked him to reconsider his goals, to consider his relationship with his wife and his children, and also, his relationship with the workplace.

I asked him to consider the hugely beneficial effects of continuing to do the things he was really good at. In other words, being a type of mentor to younger people who are very confused and lost and feeling isolated in a huge corporation. James said that he had interpreted this position as being a total failure. He would stop at nothing else but being a manager. I, in the end, had to explain that I couldn't make him what he wasn't. He had already applied for several managerial positions in the corporation and had been turned down. Each rejection was like a physical blow to James and he said that he could not stand the rejection anymore. I told him that neither I, nor anybody else, could show him how to become a person that he was never meant to be and by doing this, we would be doing him a huge injustice.

James left this session enraged, never to return. He told me that he viewed his time with me as being a total and utter failure, a total waste of his time. This experience with James forced me to really evaluate what I was doing in my work. It would have been quite easy to teach him a few tricks which may initially have fooled one or two people for one or two days. However, deep down I knew that not only would this be doing a great injustice to James, it would be doing a huge injustice to the corporation who would take him on as a manager. I could empathise very much with James' despair.

He worked in a culture which was rational, numerical, logical, linear. James was a person, in reality, who was warm, intuitive, a people person. I am sure, at a point deep down in himself, he knew that these two would never meet and yet he had chosen to battle on, trying to fit himself into that round hole while being a beautiful square peg himself. We had discussed the possibility at length, of him actually leaving the corporation and trying to embark on a different career. This was far too frightening for James. It would have meant utter failure for him. Finally, I knew that I had to honour the goals that James set himself and also, to respect his decision to leave. However, I also had to respect my own sense of integrity and my own deep belief about what my job can do and what it can't do.

Even though it may have caused deep frustration for James, I could live a little bit more easily with myself and at that point, hoped that maybe some day James will allow his real self a little room to come out and actually enjoy what he sees.

James had become enmeshed in the hierarchical system which paid little attention to how well you do your work and far more attention to who you are and what your title is. Unfortunately, also, the issue of respect caused a huge problem for James. He felt that far more respect was paid to what you did in your job and very, very little paid to how you did it. In other words, results were all that mattered and the process that achieved those results was very rarely even noticed, let alone valued.

---

What we can see from these three examples, is that in the first two, the people above took the opportunity to step back and re-examine the goals that they had set themselves. It was very frightening for them to realise that these goals weren't valid. But at a certain point, they felt that they had no option but to change those goals. In the third example, the desire to reach the goal was too deeply ingrained in the individual himself and also within the culture in which he worked.

James had never worked within any other type of corporate culture and therefore this mentality represented his whole world. Also, it must be borne in mind that James had the responsibility of financing his family. There was only one income coming into his family and he would have viewed it as been totally irresponsible and irrational of him to make any move which would jeopardise his career. However, in subsequent discussion, it came to light that his wife had actually begged him to do so, but his sense of duty and responsibility for his family was so strong that he felt that he had no option but to continue. This was James' sense of his own integrity and he had to respect and follow that.

Again, I would stress that in none of these situations is there a right and a wrong, a good or bad ending. I would simply say that each of these cases demonstrated that in different circumstances different people make different decisions and place different things at the top of their lists of priorities. It also underlines the impossibility of really defining the concept of success and the concept of failure. I have learnt that everybody I deal with has a totally different concept of these words, a concept very much inter-linked with their world view in general.

I have often heard it said that our greatest successes are our greatest failures. In many ways, Ella's failure to cope with her job and Ruth's failure to express her real self in her workplace became their greatest successes when they overcame these hurdles and found different ways of coping with their situations. On the other hand, if James is successful in gaining his position in management, the reality of management may not at all match up to his initial picture of success.

## SUMMARY

- The material image of success can be transitory. A deeper sense of success lies with our innate feelings of self-worth.

- Career sessions can offer us time out to stand back and evaluate ourselves and the contribution we are making right at this present moment.

- Every action we take is meaningful. It is wonderful to be rewarded externally for our work but even more important is the value and meaning we see within ourselves in our own work.

- We need to value the work that we are doing at the moment, to place it within the context of the greater scheme of things, before we clarify or plan for the future.

# FIVE

# "Can the Real Me go to Work?"

In previous chapters we looked at questions such as, "Which intelligence am I most comfortable using?" and "What are the aspects that most deeply motivate me in my life?" In this chapter, the question goes one step deeper and asks the question, "Who am I?" Again, this question is such a small one, but it is one that has been asked by people over thousands of years.

It has been suggested that the world of work is an environment in which we can actually express the deepest aspects of ourselves. However, if we do not engage in some type of questioning process, we may not be clear on what we actually want to express whilst we are working. I do not mean to suggest in this chapter that by working, we learn to express ourselves and know ourselves fully. However, we do have the opportunity in the workplace to discover aspects of ourselves that we may not have not realised were there.

In previous chapters, we identified natural strengths and talents. However, in my practice, I realise that each of us has a huge propensity to under-rate these natural strengths and talents. Even when we do identify them, we tend to place little or no value upon them. Perhaps we do this simply because these activities come so naturally to us. They are gifts and talents in which we involve ourselves, almost without thinking. Even when they are pointed out to us, we tend to think that these are gifts and talents that are shared by everybody around us. Sometimes we cannot understand that everybody else does not have the natural gifts that we have. We feel that because it comes easily to us we then cannot see why this activity could be of any value. Frequently I get the question put to me, "That's all very well Andrée, but what good is that in the workplace?" This is a very valid question and one that we constantly ask ourselves.

It is particularly in the area of personality, that we are presented with the stereotype that is proposed to be successful. We are given the impression that in order to be effective in the workplace, we have to possess a certain personality. In this way many of us, before entering our workplace, don a facade or pretend to have a personality that really does not reflect us at all. However, the prospect of really being ourselves at work is a most frightening one.

I remember once counselling a young man who was a natural actor. Everything in his demeanour, in his personality and in his profile suggested that he would be highly successful in this area. However, he insisted that what he needed to do was to enter the area of engineering. I was absolutely flabbergasted at his choice. He had already sat some engineering exams and failed them gloriously. I asked him did he not see that the path that he was choosing was definitely not his? Laudable as that path may be for others, it certainly was not his choice. He explained that he was quite aware of the choice that he was making. He was aware that the engineering area did not resonate with his deeper self. But he further explained:

> *"Don't you see, the area of engineering has nothing to do with the real me. I can work in this area totally impersonally. It will not impinge on the deeper me, in any way. Therefore, if I fail in this area, it has no great resounding effect. Acting, on the other hand, affects me in the deepest way. If I ever chose to fulfil this dream and do what I really want and I really love, and then failed, I would be devastated. This failure would affect me at the very deepest level. I really don't think I could ever get over that."*

He left my office determined to become an engineer. It was safer and in that way he could protect his vulnerable self. In many ways then we separate our work from our real selves as a means of protection. If we have to endure any severe criticism in the workplace, or encounter many failures, we can then successfully switch off from this "donned" self and come home to where our real selves reside and find relief and solace in that environment. Perhaps, bringing our real selves to work is a huge risk. It may be seen as dropping our protective cover. However, I have also found that because we spend so long in our workplace and we have to assume this other personality for such an amount of time in our lives, that we gradually forget what the other person is like for the short periods we spend at home.

We assume this other personality more and more and gradually lose contact with the person we really are, or the person that we once were. It also robs us of the opportunity of expressing our real selves in a public place, to see ourselves in the public realm and also to gain feedback from those around us. In the following case studies, we meet people who came to a crisis point. Their workplace demanded that they acted in a certain way. However, this method of behaviour conflicted at a very deep level with who they perceived themselves to be. In both cases, it became impossible for the individuals to continue in their past pattern of behaviour and, they were left with no choice but to instigate a huge change.

## LUKE

When he first started his careers research, Luke was very depressed and frightened. The move to a newer and bigger company a year previously seemed like a wonderful idea and the chance of a life time. Luke jumped at the opportunity. Now, a year later, it seemed that everything had backfired. What had gone wrong?

> *"I'm just not reaching my targets. I don't seem to have the skills they require. They are going to fire me, so I might as well jump before I'm pushed. Maybe it's time for me to change career?"*

Luke was a production manager in a large company and was beginning to wonder if he had studied in, and was working in, the wrong area for him. From his aptitude tests, his mechanical and numerical skills were far higher than his other skills. In his personality profile, he came across as someone who is highly detail conscious and hard working. He was practical and data rational and usually not one to become overly anxious. In his interest inventory, he rated industrial and mechanical occupations as the area which would attract him most. Overall, he seemed to be ideally suited to the job he was doing.

Yet Luke explained that he was extremely unhappy in his job. Before coming to work each morning, he would be extremely fretful, imagining all of the problems he may have to encounter. He felt that he was basically not able to cope with this position. It was his fault – he was just not able to stick the pace like everyone else. I asked him how it was for him in his last job, as he had held exactly the same position. He replied that there he had no problems. He had always reached, or even exceeded, his targets. The reason why he was offered the job by this larger company in the first place, was because his achievements were so good in his last job!

As we talked, it became clear that we would have to examine the difference culture between the two companies. The last company was much smaller and Luke would have known all of the employees to some degree. He would have had a team of technicians whom he had known for some time. They knew how he worked and he knew how they liked to work. If one of his team had a difficulty, Luke would have known them well enough to know roughly how to deal with it. If for some reason, the team did not reach their target one day, Luke would know how to motivate them to make it up the next day. He knew he could do this because he was confident of his relationship with his team. They were not working for him, they were working with him. If there was ever a problem, Luke just knocked on the door of the supervisor and had a chat – the problem was addressed there and then in a personal manner. The overall atmosphere was a busy, happy one.

His new company was much larger and therefore employed a far greater number of employees. Some of the staff were part-time and some worked shifts. Luke found that he had constantly to work with a different team. He would have just established a rhythm with one team, when the members would be changed and they would have to start over again. Luke found that he could not relate to his team and that his team found it hard to relate to their work as they kept having to change. Not being able to form any rapport between each other or any rapport with their work, the focus was placed entirely on the number of items produced. Production would be checked several times a day and the numbers had to be honoured, regardless of the circumstances of the workers. I asked Luke could he link up with his supervision colleagues and ask for their support? He replied that this was not so easy – the place was so big and so busy, that people communicated with each other only by memo or by e-mail.

We saw clearly that two essential elements of Luke's personality were not being honoured. The first was that Luke was highly empathetic. He needed to be able to relate to the people with whom he worked. He was hard working and conscientious but he also had to feel that he was part of a social unit. It was important to him that his team were happy and content in their environment and if he could do anything to help this, he would. He had a gift for recognising people's work patterns and being able to create the conditions in which they could work to their full capacity. He would also help members of his team to sort out any working conditions that needed to be addressed.

Luke was conceptual and liked to be able to perceive the whole picture. In his old company he had some links with the design team and would have had some idea of a product from its inception. He would also have known some of the customer support team and would have some idea of the level of customer satisfaction. He would have regularly made suggestions on how products could be improved. However, his new company was so big, and each department so compartmentalised, that there was rarely any interaction. Luke was only aware of his section and had little idea of the design of products or of what happened to them when they were rolled out of his section. He had made no new suggestions since joining the company as he felt that "it was not his place". The product became curiously dead for him and he rapidly began to lose any sense of excitement or even interest in it. One had to concentrate on the figures.

I pointed out to Luke the gift he had for making people comfortable and therefore productive in their workplace. Luke was singularly unimpressed at this point by his "gift" and saw it rather as being the source of his problem.

*"What good is it making people comfortable? That's not what these guys want. You have no idea what it is like today in business! They are only interested in money. They*

*are not interested in whether people are happy or whether they like their work. They give them a job and that's it. My job is to produce so many pieces per hour and I'm not up to scratch. The other supervisors get it done. My problem is that I'm too soft and too interested in people. If I didn't give a damn, I wouldn't have this problem. If I want to work in big business, that's the way it is."*

I agreed with Luke that this is the idea that this company seemed to be portraying. But just because this company is successful at the moment, does it mean that this attitude is right? I suggested that he could change, to become the person described above. He could get his production figures up. He could cut himself off. He could harangue his staff. He could see them as numbers doing a job and, yes, his figures would almost certainly exceed the target. But what about Luke himself? What about deeper beliefs he might happen to hold?

*"Is a skill like mine really appreciated?" Luke asked.*

*"It is highly appreciated by people who see its value and long term effect." I replied.*

Luke was not convinced. We sat in silence for a few minutes and decided to call it a day.

In the next session, Luke had thought about what work had meant to him. He decided that he could become what the company wanted, but it would only work in the short-term. He thought that he would become so stressed that he could not keep it up long-term. I thought it important to depersonalise this situation and to show Luke that he might not be the only one who would find this situation difficult. I asked about the teams of technicians. It seems that the workers worked under pressure. Would they work as hard when not under such pressure? Luke said it was hard to know but that one got the impression they did not like what they were doing.

I thought it significant that Luke had not made any suggestions to this company since he had joined it. There did not seem to be any mechanisms to do this. We wondered about just how many ideas this company was missing out on. The system was so strict that there was also no mechanism by which the technicians could make any suggestions on how the job they were doing could be improved. They would be the ones most qualified to suggest changes as they were working on the ground level. But there was a large turnover of staff. People could only stick it for so long. It was beginning to seem as if these systems may work on paper but on the ground they were very costly in terms of time and money spent on retraining. Could a team continue to work at this pace in an atmosphere that was not agreeable over a long period of time?

We could only guess at this answer, but we both agreed that people may not be able to and that a lot of time and energy was going into very short-term planning. Luke was beginning to see that numerical reasoning strictly applied may not always mean the most logical business approach in all cases.

Luke felt that it would only take a minor change in approach to produce rather major changes in the level of enthusiasm of the employees as a whole. He felt that if slightly more time was spent conferring with teams and creating ones that worked well together, the morale of the teams would rise considerably and productivity would be maintained in a less stressful way. The rationale behind this management approach was that things had to be done as quickly and as efficiently as possible because they were involved in a very competitive industry. But Luke felt, and had found in his former job, that if people were given just a little space, they would work with you to attain these targets. Suggestions and opinions of technicians could be listened to and respected so that people could feel that they were playing a more integral part in the company. We explored ways in which a new approach could be presented in a practical and business-like way. However, in the end, Luke felt that these approaches would be interpreted as being "touchy-feely" by the company in question and that they would possibly not implement them anyway.

We therefore focused our attention on finding Luke a position in which he could use the gifts he was now beginning to value. He was beginning to see that not only was he an excellent technician, he was also a superb people manager. He decided to look for a smaller company which would appreciate that skill and in which he could combine the technical with the personal. A company in which the team would know why they are working, what they are doing and would know that they could also have some input into the future development of the company. Once again, I felt that the original company was losing a very good man and they didn't recognise that fact through a lack of managerial skills. The particular skills which Luke had were not recognised and were not put to good use in a company that very badly needed these very skills. In the above example, Luke felt that he had no option but to leave the workplace and find a position which was more suitable for his personality.

---

However, in some cases, the work environment can provide us with the opportunity to confront problems which have been recurring over time. In short, we can decide to stick with the very distressing situation, take control of it and decide to learn from it. Paul in the next case decided to do just this.

## PAUL

*"It's wearing me down. It has been for a long time. Every morning going in there seems like agony."*

Paul was a supervisor of a team of ten people. Every morning he had to report to his immediate boss who was head of a large section. These daily meetings had become hell for Paul. His boss used the meetings as an opportunity to vent all of his pent up aggression and anger. He would constantly find a small fault in the work that Paul or his team were producing and spend at least fifteen minutes shouting, criticising and even sometimes verbally abusing Paul. This created an atmosphere of unbearable tension in the section. Everyone was so afraid of making a mistake that they focused on the possibility of making a mistake instead of on the quality of their work and thus made three times the number of mistakes that they normally would have made. There was always plenty about which their boss could shout.

Paul was a quiet person who came across in the personality profile as someone who really hated confrontation and would do anything to avoid it. It was imperative for him that he worked in an atmosphere that was calm and agreeable. He had decided that there was nothing left for him to do but to pack his bags and leave. He figured that the industry he was in, even though there were aspects of it he loved, was just too aggressive for him.

As we were discussing his profile, Paul explained that this had not been his first experience of aggression at work. It had happened a number of times. He found that he could not handle it and just froze in the face of his aggressor, wishing that they would go away. When we further examined the situation, we found that aggression had been shown to Paul, not just in this industry, but in others as well. Would a change of career really solve his problem? Paul said that it would. A change of place would mean that he could start again – it would be much better. We began to look at alternative careers.

However, in the next session, Paul took a different stance. He had been thinking about my question and had discussed it with his wife. He was sick of this constant aggression. He would just confront this bully, have a screaming match and if it came to fisticuffs, well, so be it! It had always been so embarrassing in front of his staff. The walls were thin. They were well aware of what was going on. They simply saw their supervisor as someone with no guts. It was time to save face and to do something about it. His wife had become anxious and urged caution. But Paul was fed up of being a wimp. This time he was not going to run away. His boss had no right to treat him in this manner. He had rights as an employee and as a human being and he did not deserve to be abused.

The learning had started. Paul was enjoying beginning to see himself as a person with just as much right to respect as anybody else. He had always treated his boss with respect. He had the right to expect the same in return. He was going to demand it – forcibly, if necessary!

Paul decided that the only way this man would ever listen to him would be for him to shout back even louder. He would only respect

Paul if he used force and aggression and return. Anything else would be a waste of time. I agreed that this would be a tactic and also agreed that this man would probably stop and listen to his show of strength. This man may respect Paul more. But would Paul respect himself?

There was also another aspect – this man was far better at the game of aggressive control than Paul was. He had made it his main management style and had been practising it for years. He was good at it and therefore very confident in these type of situations. If Paul adopted the same technique, he would not be able to learn all he needed to in a short period of time. I asked Paul did he believe in this system of management? He most certainly did not. He had seen the amount of damage it had caused to his staff and to himself. It had even been having a very detrimental effect on his boss, himself – he was 48 but he looked 60. We wondered then that, if this system was so damaging, why would Paul use it as a course of action?

Paul told me I had to get wise and get real. This was the way that "real" business worked. These guys only knew one language and if you did not speak it, they treated you like dirt. It was all very well for me sitting in a peaceful office. I did not see how things really were. He had tried to be himself for years but he was not accepted or respected for it. He should have taken this decision years ago. His real self was not valued here and he would have to "pretend to be someone else".

I came back to the point that Paul had made about this approach being abhorrent to him. Did he think that he would have to adopt this approach only once? In reality it would have to be done every morning to achieve the same effect. Did he think that he would only have to use this approach on his boss? His boss would then expect him to act the same way towards his employees. Did he think he could act this way all day at work and not carry it home. His boss was separated now and lived on his own. If Paul had to practice being someone else for eight hours a day, five days a week, would there not be a strong possibility that he would forget who he once wanted to be? He may also become a bully at home? Would the real Paul get lost and forget to stand up when asked? Would adopting this approach be only giving more credence to it? Would we not be saying that this is the only effective way to act in this situation? Would we be saying that business is like that, that there is nothing you can do, so accept it?

More importantly, this could be a learning situation for both of them. Paul had the opportunity to learn other, more effective skills, but also his boss may learn that his techniques are not too effective and that there is an alternative to dying from stress at 55. Paul was not too concerned about what may happen to his boss. I asked him to think about what kind of person he would like to be at work. About whether he was prepared to find another way to approach this problem and about how he would like his home life to be. His challenge was to find a way to be himself at work but yet to be able to remain in control and to command the respect from his work colleagues that was his due.

*"And how exactly are we going to do that?" Paul asked, with much scepticism.*

I told him that I did not know at the moment, but that I had total confidence that Paul had all of the capacity he needed to deal effectively and conclusively with this situation in a way which would be valid for him and which would heighten the respect that he had for himself at the end of it. Would he be prepared to stand back and give this another chance? To look at alternatives? Paul was not sure. He said that he would have to think about it. He would have to get this right this time because if he didn't, he would be devastated.

At the next session, Paul was ready to go. We had to find out first of all what exactly was happening during each session? What was the role that each of them played? Were there different scenarios or did they both follow the same script? We decided that to learn more about this situation we would try to act it out. I asked Paul about the language his boss would use and we set up a pattern. His boss's name was Dan, so we christened him "Dan the Man". I would come bursting in through my office door, shouting and using more or less the same language as Dan the Man.

At first, Paul found this very distressing. He would immediately freeze up and get very agitated. Slowly it began to dawn on him just how ridiculous I looked! I am not tall and I am relatively softly spoken, yet, here I was stomping around yelling. All my dramatics were beginning to lose their effect, so I came up fairly close to Paul's face, very quickly. He got such a fright that he backed away, unbalanced his chair and ended up on the floor. That was it, we both ended up hysterical! The next morning, however, Paul had to face the real Dan the Man. This was no act, this was the real thing! Yet, when Paul saw him first, all he could think of was me, barging around and the two of us in hysterics. He had to try and stop smiling. He began to watch Dan the Man and to see exactly what he did. This period of observation only lasted some seconds before Paul was, again, drawn into the emotional distress of the situation.

At the next session, he was depressed. "It did not work," he proclaimed. He came out of Dan the Man's office just as upset as ever. However, this way of behaving had become a habit for Paul over many years. He was not going to change it in one day. And yet he had changed it dramatically in one day. For the first time, Paul had been able to step back and observe this situation objectively, as if he had not been part of it, and had been merely an onlooker. For some split seconds, he was not drawn into the drama of the situation emotionally. For some seconds, he was in charge of his own emotional response and was not at all influenced by all the dramatic gestures of the brave Dan the Man.

We went over these few moments of calm in depth to allow Paul to feel what it was like to be in the same position as before. Paul saw that we did not have to make Dan the Man change, but that he had to first change his own reaction to the situation. This would be the only change which would have a profound effect on Paul's life. He could then command the same control in a different situation with a different person. Paul was building up skills which he could use now and in the future. In the intervening week and between sessions, Paul attended his meetings every morning. Each morning he stayed detached for a few seconds longer. It became a game for him to see just how long it could last.

Dan the Man could see that there was some subtle change. There was no point in investing so much energy into something if it did not achieve the required effect. He was supposed to shout and bellow and the person in front of him was supposed to feel totally intimated. Therefore, Dan the Man always felt in total control. He felt better about himself when in total control. But what happens when you shout and bellow and the person in front of you is getting less and less intimated? You redouble your efforts. Dan the Man worked himself up into a frenzy. Paul told me at the next session that he did not know how much more he could stand and that he would have to bail out soon.

*"What exactly is he saying?" I asked Paul.*

*"What do you mean, what is he saying? He doesn't say anything, he just picks on some small detail and goes ballistic about it. He just wants to remind me who is boss," Paul replied.*

When we thought about it, we both felt it was rather odd that someone would have a meeting each morning about one small detail. Dan the Man might have been saying something that Paul was missing amidst all the drama. Paul decided he would focus on what Dan the Man was or was not saying. He decided that the next morning, he would bring a note book and pen. Dan the Man was in flying form and in full voice. He did not notice the notebook until the very end.

*"What are you doing with that?" he bellowed.*

*"I want to make sure that I remember everything you say, Sir," replied Paul politely.*

There was a few moments silence as Dan the Man stood nonplussed in mid drama. At last, his curiosity could not bear it anymore.

*"What did I say?" he asked, in a much smaller voice.*

*"You mentioned that there was a typing error in the Brown & Associates letter, Sir."*

*"Don't be daft man, I said more than that in ten minutes!"*

Dan the Man was back to his bellow.

> *"I'm sorry Sir," said Paul, even more politely. "If you did make more points, I must have missed them. Could you repeat them so my staff and myself can make sure that they don't happen again?"*

At that point, all of his dramatic innovation completely escaped our Dan. He stood, desperately, trying to remember one more point, but failed miserably.

> *"For God's sake, man, that's your job! Be more attentive tomorrow!"*

And indeed Paul was. He came into the meeting the following day, armed with an even bigger pad. This time Dan the Man was ready for him. He was sitting at his desk with a list in front of him. He could not innovate to the same extent, as he had to make sure that he actually said something that Paul could take down. The focus was drawn away from his anger and on to business. The meeting suddenly became slightly more constructive and slightly less personal. It was also much shorter.

There had also been a change in the office staff. They noticed in the last few days that there had been little shouting in their boss's office. Paul had also been talking to some of his team and, by mistake, referred to his boss using the nickname he used. The poor man's name was instantly and irreversibly changed. Dan the Man was beginning to seem less frightening to everybody concerned. If the morning meetings were an opportunity for Dan to air his grievances, it could also work the same way for Paul and his staff. For the next meeting, Paul came armed with his own list. Dan felt that this was the height of impertinence and promptly ignored Paul's list. Paul prepared lists over a certain period, all of which were ignored. He finally prepared a list of all the requests which were denied and told Dan that if some of these were not addressed he would take them to the board of management. Dan was highly amused.

Paul hesitated over making this step and we discussed it at length. Dan could make life unbearable for all of them, if crossed. But then, could it he make it more unbearable than he had already made it in the past? Dan had played his trump card and it hadn't really worked. Paul prepared a business-like list of all the unaddressed items and also listed treatment of his staff which he found particularly offensive and unacceptable. His list was detailed, dated, specific, non-personal and factual. A meeting was called with the board of management which Dan attended. Paul was factual, objective and prepared. Dan became annoyed and attacked. The board was impressed with Paul's performance and suggested that he attend a management conference which was coming up. In the eyes of the board of management, Paul was suddenly someone who could confront a difficult situation in an effective way. They needed someone like him in another division.

Paul had managed to deal with this situation effectively without ever raising his voice. Even though he was constantly in an aggressive, hostile environment, he always chose not to join in on the game. He identified his own values and waited until he could find an effective, ethical way to deal with the situation. Because Paul remained true to himself, his relationship with his family was not adversely affected, even though his stress was at times very challenging for them. He also never compromised on the way he treated his team. They worked with him and respected him as he respected them. It was through this mutual respect that Paul had the opportunity of making a representation for them at the board meeting and eventually helped them to change their work circumstances. Not only were his values effective but his authenticity was noted and rewarded by those in a senior position.

In our last session, Paul was thrilled but a little panicked. OK, so he had dealt with this situation. But what if it did not work out in the new section? We agreed that every situation was different and some were more difficult than others. But the value of this one was that Paul now saw himself in a slightly different way. He did not feel as much of a wimp. Yes, he would still have to work on those skills as they were still not his strongest. But, he had found a novel and unique way of finding the skills to deal with one situation. He would find equally novel and unique ways of dealing with another. It would never be totally easy. Each new situation would provide its own challenges. But it would also provide new things to learn. Paul had done it once in an incredibly difficult situation. He could do it again.

———————

As mentioned at the start of this chapter, the concept of personality is impossible to define totally using psychometric tools. The specific tools used in career guidance are what are called "personality questionnaires" which ask the client to give an opinion about the pattern of his or her preferred way of behaving at work. This questionnaire is what is termed a "self-report profile", in other words, the client is asked for his or her impression of themselves. The impressions of a third party are not taken into account. In this way, the result that is gained is a self assessment done by the client him/herself. The impression of their preferred way of behaving within the workplace is compared to the response of a norm group. The results that are given are indicated more on a scale form than as a specific numerical result. It is important that this scale is not taken as a numerical indicator and is more interpreted as an indicator of the client's possible way of behaving. The results of this questionnaire are necessarily linked to the events in the person's life at the present time and cannot be taken as a definition of the way that person will behave for the rest of their lives. Normally, the results can only be taken as being relatively valid for about an eighteen month period. After that, to get an accurate description, a further personality profile must be administered.

Even when a pattern of a person's personality in the workplace is identified, it is important to distinguish what we actually mean by the word "personality". This notion can be looked at in many ways. First of all, in the workplace, we are asked to play many different roles. This role will change according to the function that I am performing, therefore, my preferred way of behaving at home may be totally different to the behaviour I choose to adopt at work. I will accept a different code of dress. I will adjust my language register and there will be modes of behaviour that would be totally acceptable in a social setting but would be inappropriate at work. In order successfully to fulfil each function, I must adapt my code of behaviour to the role that I am actually playing or the function that I am actually performing. We can ask the question is it possible to define the "real me"?

If we bear in mind that there is a distinction between the role that I am playing or the function that I am performing and a notion of the "essence" of myself, we may thereby get some idea of what we might be talking about. Even though my role and my function may change several times during the day, according to the situation in which I find myself, the core of myself, or the essence of myself, will remain relatively unchanged.

If I feel balanced within myself, even though my role and function may change several times, I will find that each of these roles or each of these functions will be relatively in harmony with how I perceive the core of myself to be. These roles or functions will simply be a different reflection or a different aspect of my core self. The problem, however, arises when my role or my function is imposed upon me – when I feel that I have to play a role that runs directly contrary to the deeply held beliefs or the internal vision of how my real self really is. In other words, the role that I feel forced to play I may find impossible to integrate with the other functions that I may perform more naturally, or with my internal vision of myself. This can be an extremely stressful situation in which to find oneself because we are constantly trying to adjust and trying to integrate this role into the rest of our personality but constantly experience a clash or a conflict within ourselves.

Possibly the most important function of careers guidance research is to come in contact with or to gain some kind of taste of who we see our core selves as being. It would be absurd to suggest that we can totally define the essence of ourselves. This search has been continued since time immemorial and it is impossible, at any point in our lives, to fully define ourselves. However, if we can still our minds long enough to gain some type of appreciation of that silence, the still and unchangeable part of ourselves, we may adopt this as a guideline for roles which we may adopt in the future.

As we saw in the previous chapter, each of the people involved found themselves placed in situations which they could no longer successfully integrate into their lives. By stepping back and examining these situations they had to adapt the role that they played in order to feel more at ease and more integrated within the situation. The final solution that they achieved could never be seen to be a permanent one. It could be described more as a constant internal monitoring process where we use this deeper sense of ourselves as a radar or a pointer which we can use to judge our comfort or discomfort in future work situations.

Even though we are expressing the notion that more of our real selves can be brought into the workplace in a more integral way, it is very important to bear in mind the point that was raised at the start of this chapter, our sense of safety and self protection. It is not always appropriate for us to reveal the deeper or more intimate side of our nature. In fact, self exposure in some situations can leave us feeling extremely vulnerable and violated. It is therefore important that we establish very healthy boundaries for ourselves in the workplace and that we can distinguish between when it is appropriate for us to introduce more personal aspects of our nature and when it may be more appropriate for us not to do so.

I have often dealt with clients who felt very aggrieved by the amount of energy they have invested in their workplace. They explain that they feel that they have given everything to their jobs, that they have given so much of themselves in their positions at work, but felt that this was totally abused by employers and colleagues. Their input was never fully appreciated. I have also dealt with clients who felt that by exposing themselves or displaying their real selves within their jobs, they actually placed themselves in a very vulnerable position.

This feeling can leave us feeling very hurt and very vulnerable. In these situations, however, we try to touch base with our real sense of ourselves. We realise that this still sense of ourselves is never affected by external events. Even though we may be feeling very hurt, very stressed, very violated and exposed, we learn that there is a deeper sense of ourselves that remains still and untouched. There is a strong sense that, no matter what event may be taking place in our lives, there is a part of ourselves that remains detached, untouched and unscathed.

## SUMMARY

- *Identifying our gifts and using them in the workplace may cause us to feel vulnerable. However, the alternative is to adopt a facade and be the person that the job requires. If we do this, we run the risk of gradually accepting this facade as being the real person.*

- *Our natural strengths come so easily to us that we tend to undervalue them. We are unable to see how they could be of any real value in the workplace. Can we see that if we are given these gifts, they are valuable and that there is a need in our community for them to be expressed?*

- *Our deeper value system may differ from the value system expressed in the workplace. The tendency is for the individual to doubt themselves and give way to the majority view, especially if that seems to be the "successful" approach. Can we learn to value our own individual values and to seek ways in which these can be expressed in the workplace?*

- *Over time, if we suppress our real selves it causes much frustration and stress. This affects not only ourselves but those around us.*

- *We are never as effective at acting a role as we are using our natural talents.*

- *Confronting questions of identity and value systems at work allow us the opportunity to define who we are and who we are not. If this initially seems a difficult thing to do, over time we live more easily with ourselves and become more honest and open in our relationships with others.*

- *Our attempts to be honest with ourselves in the workplace opens an avenue for others to do likewise.*

- *We may be called upon to play different roles within our lives, but each of these roles will reflect elements of our core selves. During the session we try to discover that still part of ourselves that is unchanging and unscathed by criticism and setbacks.*

# Six

# Work – as part of the Flow of Life

When we engage in traditional work practices, we are actually engaging in a certain structure, a certain routine by which we can plan our day, our week, our months, our years, our holidays, our families and our lives. There is a certain flow to this structure. We find that we can fall into a routine of doing certain activities at certain times of the day. This routine lends us a sense of stability in our lives. It gives us the feeling that we know what we are doing in the present and we have an idea of where our lives are going in the future. We are given the opportunity of building our identities from our workplace.

I can describe myself as an architect, a plumber, a writer. In this way, by understanding what I do, people feel that they can understand more about who I am. There is a certain complicity in this routine. Most of us have agreed that our work days will start roughly at 9 am and end roughly at 5 pm. These hours can move earlier or later but generally there is an understanding among us that the work day will be this way. This general understanding gives us confidence that we are part of a group. That we can help and be helped. That we can co-operate in the general running of the world.

What happens, however, when we step out of this flow? What happens when this routine and this structure is no longer available to us? When our present is no longer clearly defined and, therefore, it is impossible to plan our futures. Perhaps nothing yanks us so dramatically out of this flow as sickness.

For many people, this onset of sickness can be sudden and dramatic. The effects can be deep and devastating. Perhaps, the most difficult aspect of sickness is that it is so difficult to explain. Those close to us have not had the same experience. The individual has to confront the fact that, perhaps, this illness will be lengthy and that while they are ill, they cannot form part of the workplace. If we consider the workplace, it is a far wider space than our actual building. It also incorporates our friends, our contacts. Perhaps one of the most painful aspects of sickness is that, initially, we are missed in our workplace, but gradually the gap that we have left becomes closed. In that space, we become even more isolated. In my work, I have met many people who have been confronting the challenge of sickness, very often, in conjunction with other professionals. Unfortunately, a great number of people do not feel in a position to ask for help at that stage and try to confront all of these challenges on their own in their homes. I would encourage any reader who may be in this position to consider the possibility of asking for support and help.

In this chapter, I would like to deal with two people. The first is a person who is coping with the challenges of physical illness. The second person, however, had a less visible challenge in that her challenge was a psychological one. In many cases, the latter can be even more difficult to cope with as the problems and the effects are not visible and therefore one can feel even more isolated.

## KAREN

Karen had been working in a government position for many years. This had been a very safe environment for her in that she always knew what she had to do in her work and she was very expert in doing it. She gained the respect and identity that she needed for this job. She felt that she had a place in the world and earned a relatively good living. She had sometimes thought that she might change jobs. The one that she was in was very stable, but sometimes she felt that she was living in a somewhat rarefied atmosphere. She occasionally felt the need to get out there and see what was happening in the "outside world". And then she fell ill.

She was given at one point only two hours to live. In a matter of days, her life changed totally. She had to leave her home and stay in hospital for a long spell. Every aspect of her life had changed. Suddenly, people began to see her differently. They began to talk to her slowly and with great respect as they do to people whom they see as departing shortly. She tried to tell them that this should not be happening to her. She was too young – this happened to other people and it made no sense in her life at all. It wasn't really happening. She would be out of here in no time to resume her life just as it was before. They would then understand her.

But, in her heart of hearts, she knew it was happening and her situation got worse. She responded in no way to the drugs she was given. She turned to the nurses and doctors. Even though they worked so hard and gave her so much loving care, they were at a loss to save her. Time was running out. She turned to all of the things that she had learned in her life, to all of the rules and structures that had helped her before and found, to her devastation, that none of them now applied to this situation.

Karen had reached that stage in her life where she realised that she was about to embark on a journey about which she knew nothing. She was no longer a government official, or even a mother. She was someone she knew nothing about anymore. There was no safe place, no certainty to rest upon.

She tried to explain these things to her partner. She had always trusted him. He told her now to do something she knew she could not do. He advised her to let go of the rules and to put her trust in something greater than herself. To let go and trust in "Life and Living". She grew angry. What did he know? What did anyone know of her agony, of her sheer terror? He had contacted people she did not even know. She could not even pray for herself. The words she was so sure she knew the meaning of, now made no sense to her at all. And anyway, did she ever even believe them or use them? Did they really ever have a connection with her life?

Three hours stretched into six hours and then into a very long day and a very long night. But Karen was still there. She learned to hang on and to make the most of every moment, even if that moment was filled with pain. She no longer chatted to people. She talked to them. There was so much to do and not too much time in which to do it. Bit-by-bit she began to walk and move around. Her body slowly began to get stronger, but her memories and her fear took much, much longer to heal. Gradually, she realised that it was time to leave the safe space of the hospital. She was filled with terror at returning to her home. Could she cope? Could she answer the needs of her family? Could she ever, even marginally, become the person she once was?

She spent all of her time in her home. Slowly, as she began to move about, she grew confident of her home space and her family but, gradually, it was time to take her first steps outside. The first thing Karen had to do was to come off drugs. Through counselling, she could express her huge fear of letting go of the drugs which she saw now as having saved her life. What if she let go of them and all of her symptoms came back? She would certainly not survive this time. She gradually began to realise that she was bigger than her drugs and that she could take each step very slowly. This was a long process. Each cold and each slight pain that Karen experienced brought the terror back in all its psychedelic glory. It was a case of one step forward, two steps back. At last, she could trust her life without drugs but, at the time she began to explore her career, she still carried them around in her bag – just in case.

It was at this point of considering her career that Karen began to see the difference between herself as a private person and the external image she presented to people in the workplace. She explained that not only would she now have to rejoin the workplace, she would also have to rejoin the "Life Force". She explained that since her illness, she had felt very different to almost everyone around her. She would be part of a group and would really be enjoying herself and then would suddenly feel totally apart from it and totally on her own. It was almost as if the people she loved formed part of a group with which she was not familiar. Conversely, when she tried to explain these feelings, even though her loved ones tried to understand, she could never really fully explain. Her loved ones thought that the lives they were living were sure and certain. She had learnt otherwise and this knowledge filled her with fear and extreme loneliness.

Her life, as she knew it, had changed irrevocably. She may be able to reconstruct a private one, but thought that she would never have the energy or the confidence to take her place in the world outside. In fact, she had not learned to walk properly and there was no way she going to let people know that. She did not want to be seen to be different and, definitely, she did not want to be pitied. When she thought about the job that she had done for so many years before her illness, Karen felt that she was no longer capable of doing it. She explained that her place of work contained healthy people who were able to do their jobs. They had a certain system in their lives. They had things to do and places to go. Their lives, and the structures in it, made sense to them. They could see a future in their lives. They trusted this future and made plans for it. They were part of the life flow and could never see it as being any other way.

She, on the other hand, felt that she had been cast outside this flow and could never really rejoin it. Because of the intensity of her reactions and the emotional roller coaster she had embarked upon, Karen also had concerns for her mental stability. Could she ever appear as "normal" and as laid back as the others? They could have no conception of how difficult it would be for her and she would never be able to let them know. They adhered to different rules and talked about different things that they considered so crucial, but that were now very trivial to her. She tried to feign interest in what they were saying but her efforts came across as forced.

When she did try to discuss things that were of concern to her, her colleagues would find her very intense and would suggest turning to lighter topics. How could she ever integrate into the same system having had the experience she had had? Karen put off her return to the outside world even longer but, gradually, she came to realise that her sickness was turning into a convenient excuse. She could use the fact of being sick as a buffer against doing things that may be unpleasant or challenging. There was a pay-off for being sick and she was milking it for all it was worth. Karen had surrounded herself with people who really supported and encouraged her. When they informed her that she was using her sickness as a crutch, she was furious and even became a little bit more ill to just show them how wrong they were. "How would they know? They did not know what even the effort of walking was like."

However, when she was brutally honest with herself in her quiet moments, she knew they were right.

Before her illness, Karen had seen herself as a competent and capable person. The "nice" type of person who would always be willing to help. However, now since her illness, she had been constantly dependent on people, having to ask several times a day for the most basic assistance. She deeply appreciated when this was given but also despaired that there would never be a time when she could stand on her own feet and help herself. When could she ever rejoin the give-and-take of life? Karen gradually came to the conclusion that the only person who could help her, to take her place in her life, was herself. She realised that she could use her sickness and recovery to learn lessons that she may not have learnt otherwise.

She had firstly to face the fact that when she went outside, people found her so physically changed, that they could not hide their surprise. Karen had to learn to accept their surprise and shock. To not get panicked and get upset by it herself. She had to learn to present herself to people as she was and to make progress from there. She gradually met all of the people she would have known before and answered the discreet questions. Having jumped this huge hurdle, Karen relaxed somewhat and also began to look better. She decided to see all of the help she was getting from her loving friends as a blessing, as steps on her way to recovery. She even learned to ask for more than she was getting. She realised that she had never allowed herself to do this before. Asking for things was one of the most difficult things for her. She had been always the one to give to others, but never seemed to have time to give to herself. Now was the time for serious giving to herself.

She had to eat properly, sleep well, have leisurely baths. Life was beginning to be fun and it had taken a long time to learn how to really laugh again. She also had to be careful about the type of people she met. Some people, she noticed, made her feel really good and aided her progress. Others made her feel tired and despondent. She had discussed this with her "team" and they acted as a filter for her, keeping her away from the people who were not beneficial, firmly but politely. She simply could no longer afford to please other people. Perhaps the biggest challenge she had to face during her counselling sessions was her bitterness over her illness. Why did this have to happen to her? She did not deserve it. What could she have done to avoid it? She also constantly concentrated on the worst part of her illness and how it had "ruined" the life that she had before.

Karen gradually came to see that the life she had known before was in the past. No matter how much she wanted things to be the same, they could not be. There were some aspects that were the same but she needed to start making the most of her new situation. Karen put up huge resistance to this. If she let go of the past, would there be anything to replace it in the future? However, if she did not let go of her bitterness, she would limit the creation of new things in the future and yet, never be capable of living in the past. Was she willing to embrace the positive and the future? She began to see that this was the way of life, the opposite would keep her ill. Her experiences gave her the opportunity to stand back and look at her life and at where it was going. Did she really like it the way it was or did she have the courage to change it?

Over time, Karen came out and experienced life. Slowly she realised that by knowing terror, pain and loneliness, she was not separated from people. On the contrary, she now really listened to what they said and actually understood things from her heart. She had known depression, she had felt desperation and stupidity and uselessness. She could now listen with understanding, not wanting to help anymore but just simply letting the speaker know she understood. A link was formed with people that did not need to be verbalised but was instantly seen. She began to feel less bitter and lonely and more grateful. She realised that as she learned to walk, people were glad to help. It gave them time to know her and her to know them. More importantly, she did not have to pretend anymore that her life was perfect and all planned out and nor did the people around her. She began to experience a new honesty in her own life and it became contagious.

Instead of harking back to the way her life used to be and trying to recreate it, Karen began, for the first time, to look at what this experience had taught her. She began to see that perhaps what lay ahead for her in the future, was to establish a totally different means of working. She realised that, up to this point, she had formed very much a part of her organisation and had gone along with the status quo. She had, more or less, become what the people around her had expected her to become.

She now realised that there was part of her that she never had dared to express through her work. She had a wish to relate to people on a very much deeper level. She then faced the challenge of setting up a business of her own. This was quite a slow process, and it took at least two years to establish a client base. Not only was Karen challenged on a personal and business level, she had to deal constantly with the fear that her sickness may recur. As time went on, however, and her health improved, she became more and more confident that her body would support her. Indeed, as her little business slowly took off, so also did her sense of confidence in herself. Even though it took a long time and Karen suffered much throughout her ordeal, she also admitted in the end that she had learned a tremendous amount from her experience. Once she got over her resentment, her bitterness and her rage, she discovered that this experience actually offered her the opportunity to live her life the way she had always wanted to. It gave her the impetus to forsake the security of a defined organisation and to take the risk to express her deeper self through the world of work.

---

The world of work requires of us a certain level of physical fitness. Before taking up a job, we are often obliged to do a medical examination and unless we pass this medical examination, we are not offered the position. Therefore, we presume that all of the people that are working with us are in perfect health. Should we succumb to any illness ourselves, we feel there is an immediate isolation from our workplace. A physical illness is clear. We know from the outset that there is something wrong. This illness is also slightly easier to treat in that it can be seen and it can be diagnosed. It is also somewhat easier to ascertain when this illness has passed and when we are "fit" to resume our work. Therefore, normally we can say that the boundaries between fitness and physical illness are somewhat clear.

However, when we are dealing in the area of the psychological, it is extremely difficult for us to define the boundaries between what we would call "healthy functioning" and more inappropriate behaviour. Feelings of extreme anxiety might have been assailing us for quite a long time. However, it might take us a certain period to recognise that this is actually interfering with our work and our lives. The treatment of such disharmony is also wide and varied and it is difficult for us to decipher which of these treatments we actually require.

Possibly one of the most difficult aspects of a psychological challenge is to try to discover when we are actually over this and when we feel safe and secure enough to resume our work. Possibly the biggest challenge is that of the blow to our self confidence. We are no longer confident of our judgement. We question every thought we have many times over. We may seek constant reassurance from those around us and we constantly analyse our reactions to our friends and co-workers to make sure that our actions, words, decisions and our thoughts are not seen by others as been out of the ordinary or "over the top". It is difficult for us to re-enter the "norm". The following case of Lisa outlines the challenge which some of us face.

## LISA

Lisa had always been a very academically-gifted person in school. She worked very hard and always attained high grades. She was very close to her parents, her father in particular, and built up a very loving, close relationship with him. She was very attached to her home and to her locality in general. In his work, her father had to travel around from house-to-house and from family-to-family and gradually, Lisa built up a very extensive and in-depth picture of the locality directly surrounding her home. This led to an abiding interest in politics and to the dynamics which were involved in the workings of a small, tight-knit community.

Lisa was always rather shy, quiet and sensitive and allowed her father during these visits to do most of the talking. She normally stood back and played the role of observer, listening and learning as she went.

Because she did so well in her final exams, it was expected locally that she would go to college, and she complied. She went to college and did brilliantly in her degree. Because she did so well in this degree, it was generally expected that she would go ahead and do post-graduate studies. A post-graduate position for study opened up in the United States and she went and spent two years there. During this time she felt terribly alone and isolated. It totally cut her off, not only from her family and her small community but even from her country. This loneliness led to extreme isolation where Lisa would constantly question herself.

Also, because she had been academically brilliant, she told herself that she should be more than able to cope with this situation. She hid her extreme fear and anxiety and it looked from the outside as if everything was going wonderfully well. However, a certain amount of time into her study, it became clear that Lisa was not coping. She actually dropped out of her studies and came home. She was diagnosed as having had a nervous breakdown and slowly, Lisa began to see herself as being mentally unstable. As this realisation seemed to dawn on her, so did her fears and anxieties.

She did not return to her studies and for a time did not return to work. After a period of time, she took up a position which involved working with statistics and numbers and so had more restricted access to people. Lisa felt that in this position she would be under less stress. However, way back in the back of her head, there was this feeling that she was not all right, and not like other people. She saw herself as over-reacting, over analysing, looking at things too deeply, making mountains out of mole hills, being far too dramatic and far too emotional. She began to see herself as somebody who always interpreted events as crises. Members of her family began to tell her to be careful and not to over-react using expressions such as, "You know yourself, Lisa, you always over react. That's just typical you." Gradually Lisa's vision of herself became more and more different to the vision she had of people around her.

She got married and had children. However, this fear of not being able to cope still haunted her. She had a vision of herself as not being a good mother, as not being able to cope as well with motherhood as every other woman could. She had this impression that other women had the answer. That they had harmonious home lives. Because she had a past experience of a nervous breakdown, her home according to her, could never be really harmonious. Her abiding fear was that her severe periods of anxiety would return. Anytime she became slightly anxious, she thought that period was resuming. Lisa was in a prison of her own insecurities. She had completely forgotten her academic success. She forgot how well she used to do things in the past and how well she had done at her job. The only reality for her was the present, in which she felt that she could not cope with the everyday pressures of ordinary living.

We began to have a look at what really interested Lisa. She told me that her real interests were over the top. That she had concerns that other people didn't have and that perhaps she should get rid of them and basically take her life down a decibel or two. I suggested that not only should we not put a lid on these things but that perhaps we could have a look at what exactly they were and how they affected her life. At this stage, Lisa had been taken off her medication and her doctor felt that she needed no further medical attention. She was, however, attending a counsellor to whom she was very close and suggested that we would work in conjunction with this counsellor. After much discussion and much reassurance, Lisa began to describe the genuine depth of caring that she felt for each of the families that she used to visit with her father. She was passionately interested in their lives and in their welfare and explained to me in depth how she wished that the political structure could work.

When she felt a little bit more confident, I suggested that perhaps she could contact politicians in her local area. She felt she could not cope with this. Why would they be interested in her, with her track record? What good could she ever be to them? I encouraged her to try, and went over, many times, all of her gifts and all of her talents and explained that, far from avoiding her, politicians in her area would be absolutely thrilled with her participation. Lisa did not do this straight away, but waited until she felt ready.

Eventually, local elections were imminent in her area and the particular political party which interested her actually advertised for campaigners. Lisa contacted this political party and went out with a group of people to campaign. She came back to me and said that she was not very good, that she never said anything when they arrived on people's doorsteps, that she let everybody else do the talking. I countered that, indeed, I thought she was brilliant. The very fact that she had contacted this political party and had agreed to go out with that group was now opening her to the possibility of getting more involved in her community. Up to this point, Lisa had more or less isolated herself within her house. She had few contacts with people outside, simply because she felt that the atmosphere within her home was more controllable. She understood it and she understood herself within its framework. However, moving outside was a very frightening experience. I greatly admired her courage and strength to make this first move.

During this election campaigning, Lisa got to know some people in a very quiet and reserved way. But gradually, these people began to realise that she existed in their community and what an asset she was. After the election she kept up contact with the campaign office. We kept meeting and discussing what the future could hold for Lisa and gradually, we discovered that one of her interests was in the general communications area. We looked at all kinds of courses and eventually chose one. Even though the course attracted her very much, Lisa thought that she would never get the interview. Even if she did get the interview, would she ever have the ability to stay on the course? Would she have the "stickability" or would she have stability to see it through? Quite apart from this, even if she did get the course, what would she do with the children?

Lisa felt an awful lot of guilt when she considered her children. Anyway, we went through the steps of filling out the application form. Lisa was called for an interview. Then we had to broach the next barrier of actually dealing with the children. Lisa was given the name of a reputable woman and she went around to visit her. When we next met, Lisa explained to me that her gut instinct about this woman was that she didn't like her and that she would not be good for her children. But immediately she said to me, "But perhaps that's just me over reacting and over analysing? Perhaps, this woman would be really good for my child and I can't see it!"

We then had a long discussion about trusting our gut instincts, that our children are our primary concern and we are their primary protectors and that most of the information we get about our children is from our gut instinct. I was adamant about the fact that Lisa's gut instinct was just as valid as anybody else's gut instinct and that it was very important that she took not of it. "But what if I am over reacting? What if I'm wrong?" said Lisa. I replied that there was nobody who knew her children as well as she did. She could totally trust her gut instinct and if this situation seemed wrong to her and right to everybody else, it was still wrong. After some hesitation, Lisa rang the woman and told her that she would not be requiring her services. Lisa's big fear at this stage was, "If this woman isn't good enough, will I think all the rest of them aren't good enough either? Am I again just over reacting?" Again, I assured her that her instincts and her gut reactions were just as trustworthy now as they were before her nervous breakdown and that she must go with them.

Time passed and nothing happened. This was a very challenging period for Lisa. We discussed the fact that if she advertised, the right person would come along. It was really a question of Lisa having faith in the process. During this time, I really admired her strength and her patience. Finally, the result of her interview came and she had been accepted onto her course. She was absolutely thrilled but again assailed by doubts and fears. She felt that the image that she had given at the interview might have been a false one and that once the people got to know what she really was like or once they had learnt her past history, they would then be sorry to have chosen her for this course.

Again, Lisa had to learn that she could once again trust the process. If these people who were experts and professionals had chosen her for this course, then she was the right person to be on it. If she was meant to do this course, she would do it. She then began questioning what would she do once the course was over? Would this lead to anything constructive, to any type of a job? Again, I explained to Lisa that we could only take this process one step at a time. The only responsibility we had was to do the best that we can in the present moment. We could try to follow our sense of integrity and then we could trust the next step of the process. Finally, Lisa accepted her position on this course. She began her course and became very busy. For this reason we did not maintain contact with one another.

It was a full eight months later that I rang Lisa to inform her that I was thinking of writing a book and to ask if she would mind if I used her case study. She said that on the contrary she would be delighted if someone could learn something from her own experience. However, she felt that her experience was nothing out of the ordinary and nothing important. I felt that Lisa's courage and conviction were exemplary and that many people could learn from her actions and her decisions.

I then asked her, was she still on the course and how was it going? Not only was she still on the course, but the course director had organised a project by which the students would take over the programming for a week. She had been chosen to be head of the group and basically had filled in as course director for the week. I was absolutely aghast at this new confident woman I heard at the other end of the phone. In fact, when she had first started talking, I actually did not recognise her voice. I had known her voice to be rather frail and hesitant, now I heard the gentle voice of a strong woman. I tried to explain the difference to her but she could not see it. "Honestly, Andrée, I don't feel any different than I did eight months ago."

Sometimes when we are involved in a process, the changes take place so gradually that we are not even aware of them ourselves. Only people who have not seen us or met us for quite a period of time see the changes and the changes that I saw in her were absolutely amazing. She quickly explained to me that even though she was doing well, all was not rosy in the garden. There were still many challenges that she had to face each day and she constantly had to balance different factors in her life. I agreed with her that none of us had the perfect solution and that all of us were constantly balancing different elements in our lives. This was normal. This was, in fact, "Life and Living" and was a common experience for all of us.

It was wonderful to talk to Lisa and to see that this new aspect to her had finally emerged. At this point, she had not yet decided what would be the outcome of this course, and what area she would like to go into. But I felt now, very strongly, that she had found her feet. She had also built up quite a number of contacts around her and with these new found skills and her natural talents, that she would gradually work out the rest of her process, step-by-step, with great success.

---

Sickness can be considered as a catastrophe or the end of "the good life". It can be borne with much bitterness and resentment, isolating us from those around us, depriving society of our valued presence. On the other hand, our experience of sickness may be seen as the cracks in our perception of what our perfect life should be – and the light can shine through cracks! This "interruption" in our neatly planned life can open us up to deeper and broader possibilities. It can challenge us to ask questions we have never dared to ask and to question notions which we have never dared to question. By examining commonly held notions of "physical fitness" or "mental stability", we can open up to totally new interpretations of ourselves. The choice with sickness often is, "Am I going to accept the label of 'physically disabled' or 'mentally unstable' or am I going to face the fear that these notions bring up, pass this barrier and enter into a much clearer and deeper perception of myself?"

## SUMMARY

- *Illness is seen as a disaster by the majority of people and generally means exclusion from the workplace.*

- *Exclusion from the workplace means breaking with routine.*

- *Illness can provide us with a wonderful opportunity to stand back and assess our lives. The very isolation it imposes means that we are forced to forge our own identities.*

- *A mental challenge shakes our confidence in ourselves to the core. It can also produce wariness and suspicion in others.*

- *The uncertainty and isolation caused by coping with a mental challenge can again allow us to reassess our lives. It allows us to establish time for ourselves and to define what our basic needs are. We may even find that we then follow paths which we never thought of following.*

- *Sickness can be viewed as a curse or as an opportunity for learning and reassessment. If we choose to learn, this period of retreat can mark a turning point in our lives.*

# Conclusion

The whole process of career change is generally initiated by a niggling feeling that all is not as it should be. People explain that life has become routine, that it has lost its buzz and that they are merely "going through the motions".

The notion of "success" at the start of our career may have been defined by the external symbols of car, title, position and money. As we mature we assess our work using more internal criteria, aligning our interpretation of "success" more with our own personal value system. We begin to change the emphasis from concentrating simply on what we are doing to questioning who we are and why we are doing it.

We may recognise that we are not happy in our present position, but the prospect of change is a daunting one. Once we even entertain the notion of giving up our present job and looking for a new one, all of our insecurities and fears about ourselves float very quickly to the surface.

One of the main fears that we have is that we are not intelligent enough and that, while we are managing to survive in our present position, we may not be able to cope with a new one. The fear is based mainly on an incomplete understanding of the notion of "intelligence". During our formative education we are given the impression that, if we are not good with words and numbers, we are not intelligent. What is being discovered today is that the possible manifestations of intelligence are infinite. We may have taken a job having never given thought to what intelligence we might be most comfortable using. Not having done this, many people find themselves in positions where they are using intelligence with which they are not at all comfortable and suppressing gifts that would be inspirational for themselves and others.

Another fear that we hold on to is that the things that really motivate and stimulate us are impractical and that they could never be incorporated into the world of work. We may have voiced a desire to follow a certain road when we were young but have been told by an adult that these ideas were silly and that we could never make a living out of that. We may have suppressed these ideas, taken another route and relegated our original ideas to the realm of far-off dreams. We have seen examples in this book of some people who resurrected these dreams, dusted them down and gradually incorporated them into their lives and even, in some cases, into the workplace.

Perhaps the area that causes us the most concern is the question of our own identity – who we really are. One of the most frightening questions that we can ask – "Who am I?" – is frightening because we may get answers we were not expecting. We may find that our real selves and our value system does not run in accordance with the majority view. We may find ourselves at variance with the concepts of large corporations or even with the business world as a whole! The first temptation is to think that we are wrong, all of these other people could not have got it so wrong. At this stage, we just knuckle down and under. However, the questions may persist. Is there a part of me that is not at ease in this situation?

We may feel that, even if our approach is valid, how can one individual make any difference in such a large structure? We may not be understood. Would it be more effective to just act like everybody else? We may engage in this "to-ing and fro-ing" process for quite a while, before we step back and consider the questions.

When asking questions, such as "Why am I really doing this work?" or "Why am I on this earth?" we cannot expect to feed them into a computer and come out with an immediate answer. The total answer to these questions lies at the heart of the mystery of things but the attempt to answer these questions starts us on a path of self-discovery, a process which takes a lifetime. You will notice that none of the examples in this book have conclusions, all are still in the process of being worked out.

Ironically, for the majority of people the first step in defining who they are is very often deciphering who they are not. As Tony de Mello would put it: "it is more a question of subtraction than addition". By identifying the pressures, obligations and expectations which we have taken on board, but which are not our own at all, and by letting them go, we can begin to identify our real values. We can begin to see who we are by firstly seeing who we are not.

We can only begin to see the whole picture when we step back from it. In some cases we choose to do this ourselves with some help from others. In other cases, we are forced to step back. The most common means by which we retreat from the workplace is through sickness.

This can be a short-term setback which may allow us time out to draw upon our energies or to recover from stress or disappointment. But our retreat can also be a more long-term, enforced stepping-back. This can be a very challenging period in which we may run the whole gamut of emotions from abject self-doubt and depression to the zeal and enthusiasm of a medieval crusader. A period of sickness can be such a rich period of self-discovery during which we view our entire lives through entirely different eyes. It can also threaten, on many occasions, to engulf us completely and rob us of our hope and joy. It is important, therefore, that we link up with others in a similar situation, or that we put our pride aside and ask assistance from everyone around us who may love and care for us.

The main point I would like to stress in this book is that there is no single, definitive answer to careers research. It is simply a process we embark upon. This process does not take place in one day, but continues throughout our lives. A client of mine told his wife he was going for careers counselling. When he came home after the first session, his wife asked him:

> *"Well, what did she say? What did she tell you you should do?"*

My client hesitated and explained to her that he hadn't actually reached a decision yet. She threw up her hands in frustration and said:

*"You mean to say that you spent two hours with her and gave her our hard-earned money and she still didn't tell you what you should do with your life?"*

My client told me later that he found it really difficult to reply to this question and to justify the time and money he had spent on his careers research. He explained:

*"I may not yet have a concrete answer or have made a hard and fast decision, but giving myself the chance to ask these questions, of myself and for myself, has allowed me to feel more 'real' – more 'me'. I am beginning to feel more alive. I am beginning to have hope that the buzz may come back into my life. I'm actually looking forward to waking up tomorrow morning."*

# Bibliography

Boldt, L G, *How to find the Work you Love* (1996) Penguin.

De Mello, T, *Awareness* (edited by F Stroud) (1990) Font Publications.

Dooling, D M (ed.), *A Way of Working (The Spiritual Dimension of Craft)* (1979) Anchor Books.

Gardner, H, *Frames of Mind* (1993) Fontana.

Goleman, D, *Emotional Intelligence: why it can matter more than IQ* (1996) Bloomsbury Publishing.

Kahlil, G, *The Prophet* (1997) Arrow Books.

Krishnamurti, J, *On Right Livlihood* (1992) Harper.

Krumboltz, J D, *Career Belief Inventory* (1998) Consultant Psychologist Press.

Nelson-Boles, R, *What Colour is your Parachute?* (1998) Ten Speed Press.

O'Donoghue, J, *Anam Cara* (1997) Bantam Press.

Rumi, *One handed Basket Weaving* (1993) Maypop Books.

Schechter, H, *Rekindling the Spirit in Work* (1995) Barrytown Ltd.

White, D, *The Heart Aroused* (1997) The London Industrial Society.

Whitmyte, C (ed.), *Mindfulness and Meaningful Work* (1994) Parallax Press.

## PRACTICAL REFERENCES

Arundel, M, *A Guide to Post-Graduate Study in Ireland (including Northern Ireland)* (1998) Oisín Publications.

Dunne, R, *Applying to College (Ireland): a school leaver's third-level guide* (1998-1999) Undergraduate Publications.

Keenan, A, *The New CV that gets you interviewed* (1997) Wolfhound Press.

UCAS, *The Big Official UCAS Guide to University and College Entrance 1999.*

# ALSO FROM BLACKHALL PRESS

## The Interview Challenge

CORMAC LANKFORD

In a society where the number of applicants for jobs sadly outnumber the number of jobs available, it is understandable that the interview has assumed a major role in job selection procedures. In a world of highly-developed communication technologies, it is also understandable that interview techniques have become very sophisticated. The interviewee therefore has to be well-drilled and well-groomed to have any chance of being successful and will have to learn how to cope with the demands of a searching interview.

Cormac Lankford's book *The Interview Challenge* has been brought fully up-to-date, and comes out at an opportune time. It is likely to provide compulsive reading for anyone looking for a job or preparing for a specific interview. It is based on practical, real-life experience and should become a classic in the area of career guidance literature.

The sections of the book dealing with the preparation required for the different elements of an interview are marked by a pragmatic, no-nonsense approach which is refreshing and eminently practical. The book is a formidable and remarkable work of research written with a lucidity that reflects the author's mastery of the subject. It will be welcomed both by career guidance officers and job-seekers, making the task lighter for the former, and giving confidence and courage to the latter.

**Cormac Lankford** is a former Chief Executive of Young Enterprise Ireland and is a careers guidance counsellor.

130pp. ISBN: 1-901657-41-8 £7.99 pbk October 1998

# Working Women in Ireland – Your Guide to Coping with Pregnancy and Motherhood

*VERONICA CANNING*

More and more women remain in the workforce today in Ireland, for financial or career reasons, or a mixture of both. Women no longer feel the huge pressure to decide between motherhood or work they want, and are entitled to, both. Increasingly, they are under scrutiny in both spheres, facing enormous pressure to be as effective as always at work while being pregnant or while combining work with on-going motherhood.

Faced with this challenge a woman really needs a well proven set of guidelines to continue to be effective – and to be treated as such by her work colleagues. This book provides these invaluable guidelines.

The main points covered are:

• Your twelve-month pregnancy – an overview of the period on either side of the birth.
• Your personal plan.
• Announcing your pregnancy and dealing with the reaction.
• Reducing stress by effective management of your time, emotions and energy.
• Your legal rights as a pregnant woman.
• The painless return to work.
• Choosing the right childcare options.
• Successfully balancing your work and your parental role.

**Veronica Canning** is the Chief Executive of Canning & Associates, a Dublin-based consultancy. She has held senior management positions for the past fifteen years, during which time she has had two children.

106 pp.  ISBN: 1-901657-23-X £9.99 pbk          September 1998